Andrea
Bocelli
A CELEBRATION

ALSO BY ANTONIA FELIX

Wild About Harry: The Illustrated Biography of Harry Connick, Jr.

Christie Todd Whitman

Ireland's Own John MacNally (with John MacNally)

Christmas in America

A CELEBRATION

ANTONIA FELIX

St. Martin's Press New York

THOMAS DUNNE BOOKS.
An imprint of St. Martin's Press.

ISBN 0-312-25309-5

Design by Susan Turner

First Edition: January 2000

10 9 8 7 6 5 4 3 2 1

ACKNOWLEDGMENTS

I would like to thank the following people for generously granting me interviews: Edi Bocelli, Vania Cenzatti, Steven Mercurio, Claudio Desderi, Dr. David DiChiera, Ana Maria Martinez, Stefano Paperini, Dr. Leslie Jones, William Riley, Lorenzo Malfatti, Betsy Medinger, and Beatrice Meucci. My deep thanks also go to my many new friends in Tuscany, including Franco Silvi, Luigi Nardi, Jean-Claude Morel, Lorella Vanucci, and everyone at the Hotel Granducca in San Giuliano. I am indebted to Marcello Garofalo for his translating assistance and insightful anecdotes about Beniamino Gigli, and to Dr. Rosanna Giammanco Frongia for her expert translation services.

My admiration and thanks go to intrepid globe-trotting photographer Susan Turner, whose artful images bring the true spirit of Tuscany to this book, and whose patience with the author's maniacal driving on the Italian freeways went well beyond the call of duty. I extend sincere and grateful thank-you's to Tony Seidl of T. D. Media, Inc., and Peter Wolverton of St. Martin's Press for entrusting me with this story. I thank my husband, Stanford, for his careful readings, enthusiasm, and nonstop loving support. And finally, I express my love and gratitude to all the teachers who have helped me find my voice in both words and music.

Note: The sources for all quotations by Mr. Bocelli are listed in the Sources section at the back of the book.

Contents

The human voice, if it is an understanding one, [is] an almost spiritual vehicle. Isn't it the fusion of the body and the mind, a mysterious force that escapes into the air as it reveals itself?

—Jules Supervielle

Photo © Agenzia ANSA

Prelude

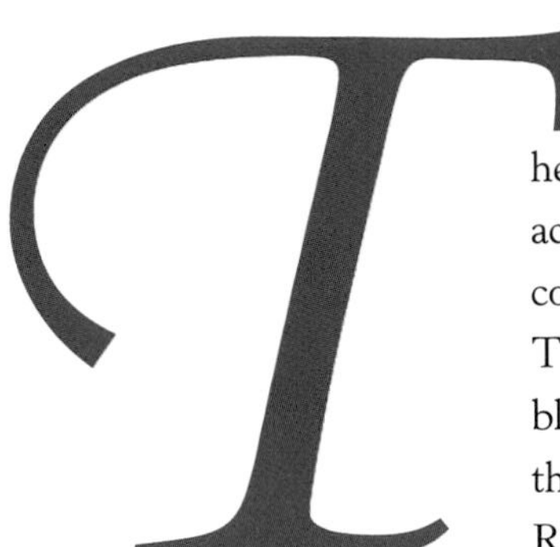

The tenor is on his knees. As the young poet Rodolfo in the first act of *La Bohème,* Andrea Bocelli is helping Mimì, played by his costar, soprano Daniela Dessì, look for the key she has dropped. Their hands are gently sweeping the floor when a sudden breeze blows out their candles. The stage lights dim, the music leads into the first tenor aria, and Andrea's heart pounds in his chest. Rodolfo's fingers brush Mimì's—his cue to take her hand and prepare to sing about how tiny, white, and cold it is in the aria "Che gelida manina" ("What a frozen little hand"). But tonight it is Mimì who is holding Rodolfo's hand. As Andrea nervously awaits his musical entrance, Dessì squeezes his hand as if to pass on the confidence she has gained in performing this opera so many times. She leans closer to Andrea and murmurs to him, *"Calmi . . . rilasciatevi . . . tutto andrà bene . . ."* ("Calm down . . . relax . . . everything's going to be fine . . .").

As Andrea's first big moment of the opera approaches, reporters and critics from across Europe wait upon his every breath. With the help of Daniela Dessi's kind and supportive presence, Andrea Bocelli forgets about the crowd and immerses himself in the aria he has loved since boyhood. Everything flows smoothly; the words, the notes, the entrance and cutoff of each phrase. When he finishes, the audience applauds warmly and the scene swiftly moves ahead.

He did it! The most nerve-wracking part of the evening is over, and his debut in a leading role is well under way.

Surviving that first aria was a turning point in Andrea Bocelli's life—being on an opera stage in a leading tenor role was the fulfillment of a lifelong challenge. For Andrea, getting back onstage for the next three acts that night was more than a test of his musicality or his stamina or his technical skills as a singer. It was a victory over obstacles that many had thought insurmountable, and that he himself had sometimes considered to be so, too. A blind person can't move on stage, they had said. A blind person can't follow the conductor or act well or interact naturally with the other singers. For a blind person, there are certain lines that will never be crossed. But after the final curtain, the encouraging applause, the raves from Andrea's colleagues and friends and family, that barrier had been crossed for good. Performing in this opera gave him another opportunity to face his fears head on and stretch himself to new limits. Tackling a leading tenor role was the latest challenge in a life filled with setbacks and triumphs.

Andrea Bocelli's native region in northwestern Tuscany is covered with gentle hills crowned by ancient towns and churches.

Inset: Andrea was born in La Sterza, a tiny village southeast of Pisa. In square miles, Tuscany is about the same size as New Jersey. There are mountains along the coast and in the east.

Photo: Susan Turner

Pisa
TUSCANY

Photos: Courtesy of Stefano Paperini

Top: Lajatico is a quiet, charming old village that appears little touched by time. The buildings, streets, and town square today look much as they did in these photos taken in the last century.

Bottom: Lajatico's town square in July 1999.

Photo: Susan Turner

1

Son of Tuscany

THE MAN WHO SINGS TO HORSES

Andrea Bocelli was born on September 22, 1958, in La Sterza, a tiny hamlet of Lajatico, which lies just up the hill. This quiet, close-knit farming community is nestled in the heart of a serenely beautiful region of gentle hills dotted with tall, elegant cedars. For centuries farmers have lived off these fields, cultivating olives, sheep, dairy cattle for cheese, and Chianti grapes for wine. The heart of Italy's Chianti region is in Tuscany, and the Bocellis have been growing their own grapes and making their own vintage, Chianti Bocelli, for two generations. Andrea describes Lajatico as a place filled with "beautiful nature, history, and simple and honest people. [It is] the place where I was born and spend my most truly relaxing times." Lajatico is located in northwestern Tuscany, fifty miles from the Ligurian Sea on the west coast where one can see the southern tip of the Apuan Alps. These mountains contain the famous marble quarries of Carrara, mined by the ancient Romans and later the source of marble for Michelangelo. East of Lajatico lie Tuscany's other mountains, the Apennines, which form the backbone of Italy running north and south. Lajatico is just southeast of Pisa and the nearby town of Lucca, the birthplace of opera composer Giacomo Puccini. To the northeast of Andrea's hometown is Florence, and to the southeast the charming ancient town of Volterra.

The first official documents of Lajatico date back to 891, and the castle in the village was built in the eleventh century. Walking the ancient streets and crossing the small, bustling piazza gives visitors a sense of intruding upon a place that has been little touched by time. Modern details such as a bright white ambulance or the small roar of a Vespa are dwarfed by the timelessness of the burnished-brown buildings and narrow, winding streets. Near the town square is the Church of San Leonardo, where Andrea and his family attended Mass in his youth and where he was married in 1992. Built in 1275, the church was enlarged in the mid-1800s to make room for a parish that had grown significantly in six hundred years. The interior of San Leonardo is covered with beautiful art, including a ceiling painting of the Virgin Mary floating among the clouds and flanked by two angels who cling to her white robes. To the left of the altar, placed inside an arched recess, is a costumed statue of the Virgin and Child. A more unusual work of art is found at the back of the church, near the east door. Set into a small cave made of stone is a miniature reproduction of the grotto in Lourdes, France, where the young Bernadette received her famous visitations from the Virgin.

Lajatico's mayor, Stefano Paperini, describes his town as "agricultural with some

This page: The Church of San Leonardo in Lajatico, where Andrea Bocelli attended Mass as a child and where he was married in 1992. Built in the 1275, the church was enlarged in the mid-1800s to accommodate a larger parish.

Facing page, top: The altar in the Church of San Leonardo.

Facing page, center: Near the back door of the Church of San Leonardo is a miniature reproduction of the grotto in Lourdes, France, where the Virgin Mary appeared to the young Bernadette Soubirous.

Facing page, right: Stefano Paperini, the mayor of Andrea Bocelli's home town, seated in his office in front of a photograph of him and Andrea.

Photos: Susan Turner, Antonia Felix

commercial business and craft activities." He says, "There are some tourist structures in place—agricultural tourism—but it is mainly agricultural, producing goods such as quality wine, oil, and cheese." He adds that Lajatico is famed for its handcrafted Irish lace. Seated behind his desk near a large photograph of himself with Andrea Bocelli, the forty-something mayor recalled his friend Andrea as a small boy playing in the town courtyard with all the other children. "When Andrea was younger, he did everything here; bicycling, soccer," he said.

Near the church, a winding, tree-lined road leads down to La Sterza. Andrea and his younger brother, Alberto, grew up in a large stone house on La Sterza's main road, facing a wheat field that borders the hill leading to Lajatico. The windows of the gray stone house are covered with bright red shutters, and the patio that leads from the kitchen door to the backyard is covered in terra-cotta tiles. On the patio, beneath the open sky, is a huge stone table, and a five-foot hedge lines the property along the road. The old family cat, a battle-scarred black male with one back leg missing, can be found stalking mice in the hedge or sunning himself on the patio. "We didn't name him," said Andrea's mother, Edi. "We just call him kitty." The grandmother of Andrea's two sons, Edi Bocelli has set up a swing set in the yard, and a plastic ball and other toys are scattered on the lawn. "This is a great place to live," she continued, "because there is no crime. We don't have drugs, and our youth are all hard-working people. So it's an ideal place to come to in Italy and travel from, to enjoy all our great works of art, our museums, everything, all in complete tranquillity. Even for women traveling alone, they can come with complete peace of mind."

DESCRIBING ANDREA'S HOMETOWN OF LAJATICO, HIS MOTHER, EDI BOCELLI, SAID, "THIS IS A GREAT PLACE TO LIVE, BECAUSE THERE IS NO CRIME. WE DON'T HAVE DRUGS, AND OUR YOUTH ARE ALL HARD-WORKING PEOPLE."

Behind the house is an orchard of olive trees and Chianti grapevines that fills a pretty half acre. On the other side of the orchard are two stone buildings that house the fami-

The old stone house in La Sterza where Andrea and his brother Alberto grew up. The house faces a lovely wheat field, and an orchard of olive trees and Chianti grapevines stretches along the side of the Bocelli property.

Photo: Susan Turner

Top: The front-gate entrance to Sandro and Edi Bocelli's home.

Left: The Bocelli's unnamed, battle-scarred cat, sunning himself on Edi Bocelli's patio.

This frame: Andrea's mother, Edi Bocelli, in the front of her house.

Facing page, top: Sandro and Edi Bocelli's Chianti orchard.

Facing page, bottom: The office of architect Alberto Bocelli, Andrea's brother, in La Sterza.

Photos: Susan Turner

ly businesses. Alberto, Andrea's brother, is an architect who specializes in restoring old homes and villas in the area, and their mother works with him on these projects. Edi and her husband, Sandro, also own a farm machinery business. They inherited the agricultural equipment store from Andrea's grandfather, and they have done very well selling tractors, combines, and other items to the farmers in this part of Tuscany.

Near the house, about one-half mile away over a small hill, is Andrea's home. Set on a narrow gravel road that leads to a string of farms, the large stone house stands in front of a stable that Alberto built for his brother's prized Arabian horses. Across the road from the house is a sloping meadow of tall grass, and to the south of the house is a thick orchard of olive trees. These are the same country roads, fields, gardens, and orchards that Andrea knew as a child. He remembers the colors of the hills and the sky and the looming shapes of rolled bales of hay in the fields. "My childhood was happy," Andrea says, "and the images I keep of it also. I loved the green of the Tuscan country, the blazing yellow of the sun. . . . As a little boy I could still see pretty well. I could separate colors very well, but not forms." His mother urged him to concentrate on the colors around him, to make a clear picture of them in his mind that he could call upon when his sight was completely gone. She knew the day would come soon.

Edi and Sandro Bocelli noticed Andrea's eye problem soon after he was born. Whenever he was in the sunlight he cried, and his eyes often became irritated and red. The first doctors they visited about the problem waved it away as nothing serious. But as their son continued to suffer, they traveled to a famous specialist, Dr. Galenga, in Turin, about two hundred miles away. This doctor gave them the grave news that their son had glaucoma, and that the condition would gradually make him completely blind. There was no hope that it could be cured, but surgery could slow down the process and give him a few years of precious sight. Andrea's glaucoma was a rare, congenital type, but no one could recall it ever being in the family before. "I was born with a hereditary

Photos: Susan Turner

This page: Andrea's old, renovated stone home in La Sterza lies about one-half mile away from his parents' house. A large stable in the back was built for his six Arabian horses. Andrea, his wife, and their two sons divide their time between this house and another, which lies on the west coast of Tuscany in Forte dei Marmi. They also own an apartment in Monte Carlo.

Facing page, top: Another view of Andrea's country house in La Sterza

Facing page, bottom: Olive trees and Chianti vines grow in a large orchard next to Andrea's house in La Sterza.

form of glaucoma," Andrea said in 1996. "From whom I inherited this disease has been a puzzle ever since, for in our family the disease does not appear at all."

The Bocellis decided early that they would do everything possible to prepare Andrea for life in the real world and not spare him the pain and tears that would help him live a normal life. "We wanted to make a man, not a handicapped person," said his mother, an energetic and robust woman with a thick shock of short white hair. "For Andrea there was no hope and I didn't want to deceive him." They agreed that their son would not be coddled or allowed to take the easy way; rather, he would face every trial and learn how to believe in himself and walk in the world with confidence. "I had to rule out pity; I had to

This frame: Andrea, top, at five years of age with his baby brother, Alberto.

Center: Andrea, two years old. As a baby he endured twenty-seven eye operations, the first of which was performed when he was six months old.

Right: Taken during the party following Alberto Bocelli's first communion, this is another photograph from the Bocelli family album. In the back row are Sandro and Edi Bocelli, the boys' parents. Alberto is third from the left in the front row, poised to cut the first slice of his cake, and Andrea is at the far right in the back.

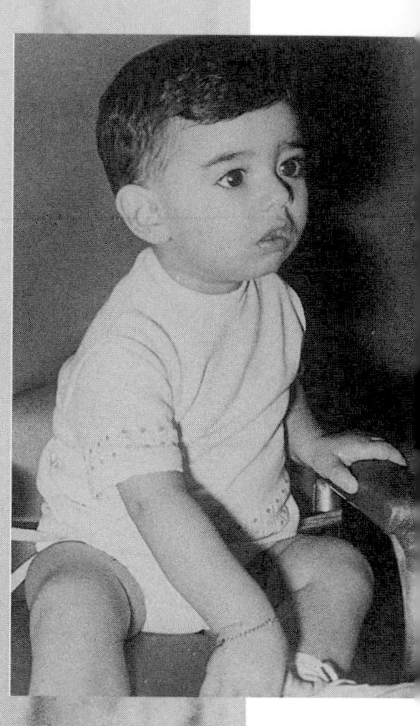

force such strength within myself," said Mrs. Bocelli. "It was terrible because it was almost impossible not to feel pity in front of that vivacious young boy who was like quicksilver, alive." She watched his eyes grow more empty every day and willed herself to not break down in tears and tender pity for him. "I would have made him a victim, I kept telling myself."

Sando and Edi Bocelli agreed always to be direct and honest with their son. They would face reality with him and never try to cover up the truth or create false hopes. If they taught him to develop his own way as a nonsighted person, they believed, he would create a unique relationship with the world that they would probably never understand, but that would serve him well. For example, when Andrea was looking out the window in the direction of a neighbor's house one day, he asked his mother if he would be able to see it when he got older. "You will never see it," she told him, "but you will see other things that we will not be able to see."

Andrea underwent his first eye surgery when he was six months old, and over the next few years the Bocellis traveled to Turin for twenty-six more operations. In Andrea's condition of congenital glaucoma, the drainage system in the eyes has not developed properly. The fluid that is constantly produced by the eye builds up and causes pressure on the

> ANDREA UNDERWENT HIS FIRST EYE SURGERY WHEN HE WAS SIX MONTHS OLD, AND OVER THE NEXT FEW YEARS THE BOCELLIS TRAVELED TO TURIN FOR TWENTY-SIX MORE OPERATIONS.

optic nerve. The optic nerve, which cannot be restored or replaced, eventually fails completely. Edi Bocelli observes that glaucoma was "not well known about" when her son was born in 1958. Today, microsurgery, laser surgery, and medications have greatly improved the chances of controlling glaucoma, but these methods must be begun in the earliest stage of the disease. There is no cure for glaucoma, there are only methods to control it that have to be maintained for a lifetime.

It was in the hospital in Turin that Edi Bocelli discovered Andrea's attraction to music as well as the powerful influence it had on him. During one visit they stayed in a room next to a Russian man who played classical music on a record player all day long. He was in the hospital recovering from injuries suffered in an explosion that had blinded him. Little Andrea turned toward the music and kicked his feet, swinging his little legs to the rhythm. As long as the music played he faced the wall through which it came and banged his feet. The music distracted Andrea from his pain and from the frightening atmosphere of the hospital. This natural response didn't surprise his mother, who comes from a family of good voices.

When they returned home, Edi bought some opera and classical albums and discovered that this music would calm her child. Andrea later said, "My mother told me that, as a baby, whenever I heard classical music I stopped crying. . . . I think that the first record that I heard was just opera—maybe it was Mario Lanza—and my mother told me that I was really impressed with these great voices." The opera record touched something deep in the boy, and he instantly felt that he had found something very important. "I don't remember who was singing," he continued, "but I realized at that moment that it was the means I wanted to express myself with." The boy was moved to tears as he listened to the singer. The emotion, the beauty, the intimacy of the voice went straight to his heart and he couldn't think of anything more wonderful for a person to do.

Photos © Franco Silvi

Top: Andrea's parents, Sandro and Edi, in their home in July 1999. They own an agricultural machinery business in La Sterza that sells tractors, combines, and other farm equipment to the region's farming community.

Bottom: Andrea's mother, Edi, in her home in La Sterza near a display featuring Andrea, Alberto, and their families. From the moment they learned that there was no cure for Andrea's glaucoma, Edi and Sandro decided to do everything possible to raise him to be "a man, not a handicapped person."

Soon everyone in the family knew that Andrea loved classical music, and his relatives began to buy him recordings as birthday gifts. They always asked him to sing, and eventually he transformed the step in front of the kitchen fireplace into his own little theater.

"It was my first stage," he said. "They would make me stand there and after all of them insisting, they would convince me to sing." Month after month, year after year at family gatherings Andrea would be asked to sing. He often says that singing is a career that other people decide for you because they bring it out, they demand it of you. The motivation to have a career as a singer comes from feeling a sense of responsibility to bring your talent to people who enjoy it. "When I was a child," he said, "everyone asked me to sing. Step by step I was understanding that that was my destiny, to sing."

When Andrea was old enough to begin elementary school, the Bocellis searched the entire country to find a place that was compatible with their ideas about raising a blind child. They finally discovered a school for the blind that impressed them in Reggio Emilia, about seventy-five miles north of Lajatico, between Modena and Parma. The school is set in an ancient town filled with Renaissance art and architecture, including a thirteenth-century duomo—a dome-capped cathedral—and a town hall from the same century that contains a special room devoted to Italy's tricolor flag, which was declared the official flag of Italy in the town square in 1797. Although Reggio Emilio was not close to Lajatico, it was on the main railroad line and had many museums and markets to visit in case Edi wanted to spend a few minutes away from the school.

One of the first strong, positive impressions of the school stemmed from the director herself, who was blind. Sandro and Edi Bocelli spent hours in the office, classrooms, and playground observing how she treated the children and how they responded to her. There was great respect on both sides, and that was exactly what they were looking for. At first

Edi wondered how a blind director could keep track of an active child like Andrea, but the more she observed the situation the more confident she became that this was the perfect place for him. "That lady saw more than anyone else," she said. "The children listened; she didn't miss a thing."

Andrea's parents were relieved and delighted to have found a school where Andrea could be challenged and respected. They enrolled him, and he began to learn to read braille and to play team sports such as soccer, which he loved. Knowing how much his grandson loved animals, Andrea's *nonno* (grandfather) bought him a pony named Stella (Star) at about this time. At age six Andrea was already confident in the saddle, and later his parents sent him to an exclusive riding academy in an area of Tuscany called the Maremma. This lush, pine-filled region along the southwest coast is renowned for its unspoiled beaches and dunes, wild boars, and falcons. Alternating between the fresh sea air and the cool forest, Andrea learned how to train horses. He loved the demanding discipline of the riding school and immersed himself in the physical and mental strain of the work. His mother recalled that there were two styles of horse training available to him: one involved *le botte,* hitting, and one involved *la bontà,* kindness. "Andrea chose kindness," she said.

> EDI BOCELLI RECALLED THAT THERE WERE TWO STYLES OF HORSE TRAINING AVAILABLE TO YOUNG ANDREA: ONE INVOLVED *LE BOTTE*, HITTING, AND ONE INVOLVED *LA BONTÀ*, KINDNESS. "ANDREA CHOSE KINDNESS," SHE SAID.

Photo: Susan Turner

Lunging the horse from the center of a ring, becoming sensitive to the horse's instinctual needs, finding his own individual style of communication with the horse were all part of Andrea's training in the Maremma. "Horses were so important to me," he said, "they were an encouragement, a challenge, and a stimulation. I spent fantastic moments with them."

Learning to ride helped Andrea feel physically free; the exhilaration of moving on a horse allowed him to race forward in space without developing any tension in his body. Betsy Medinger, a riding teacher in Connecticut who specializes in teaching blind and visually impaired children, believes that this is one of the most positive aspects of learning to ride. "The biggest thing I see in my students is the sense of freedom, emotionally," said Medinger, head instructor of Pegasus Therapeutic Riding. "Self-esteem also comes into play—they learn early on that they can do anything. Visually impaired kids lean forward and put their arms around the horse's neck instead of just petting it. They want to smell the horse and rub their faces in the horse's mane rather than just using their hands. My students ride sideways, backward, and on their tummies to get all the input and exploration that they can. The tactile situation, the relationship with the animals are integral parts of the early training, and the idea that these kids can go for a walk through the woods on a horse changes their lives. They love it, especially in the fall when there are

Gisele, Andrea Bocelli's Arabian, in the pasture at the singer's home in La Sterza. Andrea once owned six horses, but sold five of them when his schedule began to take him away from home for long periods of time. Andrea was given his first pony, Stella, by his grandfather when he was six years old, and he immediately began learning how to ride and train horses both at home and at an exclusive riding school in southwestern Tuscany.

leaves underfoot. They notice smells and distant sounds that the rest of the riders, including myself, ignore or take for granted."

With a natural love of horses and lifetime of experience with them, Andrea Bocelli is deeply sensitive to their personalities. "I hear them, I understand them," he said. He sings to his horses in order to feel whether they respond with interest or with tension. If they respond in an anxious or negative way, he knows that something's wrong—he's too tense, too self-conscious. Testing out a new song or aria in the ears of one of his horses is a unique Bocelli method that speaks volumes about his instinctive approach to music. He listens for the slightest response. "At the smallest sigh, I know everything has to be started all over again."

Andrea is passionate about Arabians, a breed that has kept pure bloodlines for more than four thousand years. The Arabian is known for its elegant size, slightly smaller than that of other thoroughbreds; for stamina that allowed the Arabian nomads to ride them across the desert; and for its affection and intelligence. Edi Bocelli recalled that Andrea's oldest horse, Jazir, was a "sumptuous" Arabian and the most beautiful in his stable. "I consider the roaring and neighing of a horse a beautiful noise," Andrea said, "as well as the humming of the wind when you gallop. What also attracts me is the concentration that is necessary for horseback riding. You can be occupied only with this, otherwise you'll make a mistake. For those who sit in a saddle, there are only two things: him- or herself and the horse. All the rest—the career, the bustle, the stress—vanishes in the background. After a ride I am often tired to death, but mentally totally relaxed."

From horseback riding to singing for his family to watching his little brother grow up, Andrea's childhood was happy—in spite of the relentless progress of his glaucoma. Then, when he was twelve, a drastic accident on the soccer field finished in an instant what the disease might have taken a few more months or years to do. The soccer ball used by the boys at the school in Reggio Emilia contained special metal plates that allowed the ball to be heard when it was kicked. Suddenly a ball came toward Andrea and hit him in the face and one of the steel plates struck him directly on the eyes. In the chaos that followed, Edi held a towel on Andrea's eyes to stop the bleeding. To make matters worse, they couldn't rush home by train because there was a rail strike. Edi couldn't get a taxi, either, but she did find a bus that was going in the direction of Lajatico. During the trip Edi continued to hold the towel over her son's eyes, and a lady sitting nearby could not keep herself from staring. She looked at Andrea and shook her head, saying, "The poor little thing, the poor little thing." That was all it took for Edi to snap. The stress of Andrea's terrible accident, the delay in finding a way home, and now a weepy woman covering them with pity—that was too much. Edi blew up at her. "She probably thought I was a madwoman," said Edi, "but on this [matter of pity] I was unapproachable. I have always been like this."

The powerful blow to Andrea's face resulted in a brain hemorrhage, and when he recovered from the injury he was completely blind. Andrea does not look back on the accident as a tragedy that changed the course of his life. His parents had been very honest about the fact that he would eventually lose his sight, and he was prepared for the loss. He realized that the accident just "sped up the inevitable." To this day he does not like to talk

This frame: Andrea Bocelli singing "O sole mio" in his first singing contest at age twelve.

Bottom right: After Andrea wins first place in the singing contest, well-wishers rush to congratulate him.

Bottom left: Song contest winner Andrea Bocelli with bandleader Maestro Maravilla in Viareggio.

about his blindness in terms of a handicap; he was raised to live a full, rich, normal life as a nonsighted person. Before journalists interview Andrea they are given a printed statement from his manager indicating that the artist will not discuss his blindness. It's not a subject that he considers worthy of discussion because he's not interested in compassion or in dwelling upon something that to him is normal, not a handicap. "The tragedy," Andrea has said, "is that people continue to make a fuss about something *they* consider to be tragic, not I."

One of the good times in Andrea's twelfth year took place in Viareggio, a picturesque resort town on the sea. Sandro and Edi registered Andrea to enter a local singing competition hosted by a bandleader called Maestro Maravilla. The room was set up nightclub style with the audience seated at small round tables, and Maravilla's small orchestra accompanied the amateur talent. Andrea cut a tall and lanky figure on stage in a light cotton suit with short pants—worn with white knee-socks—and sporting a stylish pair of dark sunglasses. He stole the show with his rendition of "O sole mio" and took home first prize, the Margarita d'Oro (Golden Margarita). This award enabled him to enter a bigger competition, the Festival of Castrocaro, but his parents and relatives agreed that he was too young to compete in such a festival.

Everyone in the room was impressed with young Andrea Bocelli that day. No one imagined, however, that one day he would record "O sole mio" on an internationally best-selling album and sing the song throughout the world in stadiums filled with thousands of people. No one, except perhaps Andrea, who already felt that his destiny lie in his voice.

When Andrea finished elementary school, his parents looked throughout the country for a *scuola media* (junior high school) that offered music courses. Andrea had been taking piano lessons since he was seven years old and wanted to explore other instruments. In Bologna they found the Istituto Francesco Cavazza, a school for the blind that allowed students to study music and singing in addition to regular academic classes. At Cavazza Andrea took his first lessons on flute, saxophone, and guitar, instruments he loved but admits he did not learn very well. "I always had an extraordinary fascination with musical instruments when I was a child," he said. "I spent a lot of money to buy all sorts of instruments, but more than playing them, I mistreated them." While he was studying at Cavazza, Andrea also spent a lot of time writing his own songs.

Musicians who are blind or visually impaired have the option of learning to read music with the braille music code. Using the same six-dot system as literary braille, the braille music code uses the dots like a different alphabet. When Andrea was once asked by a reporter how he learned his opera roles, the singer informed him that opera scores do exist in braille. To a sighted musician who has never studied braille, the complexity of reading the music code seems overwhelming. To

The Istituto Francesco Cavazza, a school for the blind in Bologna that Andrea attended in his first year of junior high school. His parents chose this school because in addition to academics it offered courses in two subjects Andrea loved: music and singing.

Photos: Susan Turner

read a piece of piano music, for example, the pianist begins reading a line of braille from left to right. There is a separate sign for every aspect of the first note, such as, "it is in the fourth octave, it has an accent, it's a quarter note, it's going to be slurred with the next note, the tempo is allegro, the dynamic is forte, and you use the second finger." All this information, read horizontally, describes one note, played with the right hand. A sighted pianist will read this information on a staff of music in one glance, and know what to play with the left hand, too. But musicians who are blind from birth do not understand the concept of a musical staff. Learning the braille music code is not more difficult for them than learning to read music on the staff is for sighted children. It's just a different system that verbalizes the musical notes rather than shows them as images on a staff.

While Louis Braille (1809–1852) was creating his literary and musical codes, which have now become standard throughout the world, other versions of music notation for the blind were being developed. Most of these systems used raised, embossed letters and numbers (rather than Braille's code of dots), and some used raised shapes similar to the notes of traditional printed music. The problem with these systems was that they could not be *written* by a blind person. A practical system would have to work both ways, giving visually impaired musicians a language in which to write and copy music as well as read it.

Blind and visually impaired singers can learn arias from operas in music books that use the braille music code. The tenor aria "Che gelida manina" from *La Bohème,* an opera Andrea performed in Italy in 1998, is printed in two or three lines of braille code stacked on top of one another. The top line contains the words to the aria in the original language,

Photo: Maple Communications

A braille music score of the tenor aria "Che gelida manina" from La Bohème. *Andrea Bocelli included this piece on his album* Aria *and performed the entire role in Italy in 1998. Braille music is a verbalized description of individual notes, in contrast to the visual system of reading notes on a musical staff. The aria in the photo is resting on a much larger braille book that contains one-half of the libretto (text) of Verdi's* La Traviata.

Italian. The line beneath that, if it's a dual-language edition, contains the translation. Both of those lines are in literary braille, but the bottom line containing the music is in the music code. Unfortunately, the braille words do not line up with the notes. The singer usually has to listen to the aria or song to learn where the words belong in the music.

"Teaching piano to blind and visually impaired students is no different than teaching sighted students," said Dr. Leslie Jones of the Lighthouse Music School in New York City. "Since I began working here I have found that my teaching is really very much the same." Dr. Jones is the director of the Music School, one part of the Lighthouse organization, which has provided early childhood classes, youth and adult education, counseling, and other services for the blind and visually impaired in New York since 1913. "The method in which these students learn their music is very different, of course," she continued, "but once it's memorized and they come in for a lesson we work on the same things that all piano students work on, such as fingering and technique." She admits that her students are excellent listeners, both while studying music and when she's working with them during lessons. Their listening skills are not "automatic," however; they're the result of hard work. "Some of my students are so wonderful because they do listen more carefully," she said, "but it's a mixed up idea that people who are visually impaired automatically have ears that are so much better. That's not true. Just like anybody who's sighted, you have to train your ears to be good. If you are blind or visually impaired, your hearing is heightened because you're used to depending on your ears exclusively. Your focus on hearing is heightened. There's more of an intense audio focus, and it improves. When you get into that groove of having to memorize music all the time, you get better at it. My students memorize music more quickly than sighted students I've worked with because they've become very good at it."

LOOKING BACK, BOCELLI IS GRATEFUL FOR THE SPECIAL BOARDING SCHOOLS HIS PARENTS SENT HIM TO, EVEN THOUGH IT WAS SOMETIMES PAINFUL TO BE SO FAR FROM HOME. "I BELIEVE IT WAS A WISE DECISION MADE BY MY PARENTS," HE SAYS, "BECAUSE I WAS ABLE TO BUILD AN EDUCATION THAT GAVE ME THE ABILITY TO CONFRONT THE REST OF MY LIFE."

The high-tech computer age has brought fantastic changes to braille music. With special computer keyboards, music can be written in the braille music code and printed out in a ready-to-read, raised-dot format on a braille printer. This speeds up the process of providing music for schools, choirs, and individual musicians. In the past, braille music was transcribed by hand and proofread by braille music specialists, of which there were only about twenty in the United States at any given time. Now, state-of-the-art translation software can also transform braille music into traditional music notation used by sighted people.

Andrea Bocelli took piano lessons on and off throughout his childhood, but not until he entered the Cavazza Institute did he get to study music with other students. At Cavazza, he was also able to take voice lessons for the first time, and he signed up for as many music and voice classes as the rules would allow. At the end of his first year, however, the school policy changed. Much to Andrea's disappointment, students were no longer able to take both music and voice classes. Instead of returning to Bologna the following autumn, Andrea stayed home and went to a local junior high with his old friends. The Cavazza Institute was the last school for the blind Andrea would attend.

Cavazza's most famous alumnus returns to the school to chat with the students whenever he is in Bologna, which is once again an important city in his life. His management company, MT Blue's, has its office there, and Andrea recorded his albums *Romanza* and *Sogno* at Bologna's Clock Studio and Fonoprint Studio. In the introduction to an interview Andrea gave to the Cavazza Institute's journal, *Vedere Oltre,* it is noted that "the availability of the artist for his friends at Cavazza is infamous."

Looking back, Bocelli is grateful for the special boarding schools his parents sent him to, even though it was sometimes painful to be so far from home. "I believe it was a wise decision made by my parents," he says, "because I was able to build an education that gave me the ability to confront the rest of my life. Not just the scholastic part of my life, but the practical part of my life."

Sandro and Edi Bocelli had taken great care and spared no expense in finding schools that would give Andrea this secure foundation. He grew up with the confidence and freedom to develop in every area that interested him, from sports—soccer, swimming, horseback riding, and bicycle riding—to reading, which he admits is an obsession. When he was at home with his family during the summers, the church played a role in his life, too. Every Sunday, Andrea went up the hill to San Leonardo where sometimes he played the organ, sang in or accompanied the choir, and listened to the liturgy of the Mass.

Edi Bocelli has described herself as a person of strong faith, and the Bocellis' religious life centered on the Catholic Church. An event from Andrea's childhood reveals the depth of his spiritual life at a young age. During a visit to a holy shrine where healing miracles have taken place, Andrea showed a quality of his character that has remained with him to this day. It's a quality that may explain part of his appeal to audiences, his extraordinary ability to draw people in.

When Andrea was eight years old, he and his family went on a pilgrimage to Lourdes, France, with a priest who was a friend of the family (and who would later marry Andrea and his wife). People have been traveling to Lourdes since 1858, when a fourteen-year-old girl named Bernadette Soubirous began to see apparitions of Mary. The celestial lady of white light spoke to Bernadette in the local dialect, and Bernadette referred to her as

Aquéro, "That one." The lady called herself "the Immaculate Conception," and in the course of the eighteen visitations a spring began to flow from the floor of the grotto. As word of the apparitions spread, the crowds grew larger and group pilgrimages from parishes throughout Europe were organized. A large basilica was built on the site to fulfill a request given by Mary in one of the visitations: "Go tell the priests that people shall come here in procession and that a chapel shall be built." After a long investigation into the apparitions and the miraculous healings attributed to Lourdes, Bernadette was canonized as a saint in 1933, fifty-four years after her death.

"I AM PHILOSOPHICALLY A BELIEVER," HE SAID. "I'VE ALWAYS THOUGHT WITH A STRANGE CERTAINTY THAT THE WORLD IS A MANIFESTATION OF AN EVIDENT INTELLIGENCE. THIS IS MY BELIEF."

Each year, about five million people from all religious backgrounds visit this shrine in southwestern France. Many come in groups, carrying banners that identify their church or organization, others come with a family member or friend who is ill. Some come out of curiosity after having read the popular book or seen the film *The Song of Bernadette*, and others come for spiritual renewal. Beyond the grotto and the basilica are low green hills that seem to insulate Lourdes from the rest of the world. The area around the shrine is filled with a sense of tranquillity and goodwill, even though the crowds number in the thousands and the narrow streets are packed with small shops selling every religious article imaginable.

This frame: The Rosary Basilica of Lourdes, France, built over the grotto where Bernadette experienced visions of Mary in 1858. The Bocelli family made a pilgrimage to this famous shrine when Andrea was eight years old; When Andrea visited the grotto, he made a suprising request of the Madonna.

Inset: The grotto where the apparitions took place in Lourdes. A statue of Mary has been placed in the area where Bernadette saw her. Every year, five million people visit this grotto for inspiration, healing, and spiritual renewal.

Right, top: The grotto at night.

Right, bottom: A candlelight Mass at the Basilica.

Photos: Susan Turner

Photos © Franco Silvi

In the evenings thousands of people gather in the large plaza in front of the basilica for the candlelight Mass. Around the corner from the front of the basilica is the grotto where the apparitions took place. Throughout the day a slow yet constantly moving line of people, some in wheelchairs, enters the shallow indentation of the little cave. A statue of Mary stands above them on a small natural platform in the spot where she appeared to Bernadette. The visitors close their eyes to pray and often touch the wall or lean forward to kiss it as they walk through.

During the Bocellis' visit here in 1966, eight-year-old Andrea and the priest walked into the grotto together. After they exited, Andrea told his friend that he hadn't asked the Madonna to restore his sight. "What did you ask for?" asked the priest. "Serenity," answered Andrea.

Edi Bocelli believes that the Madonna did give her son serenity that day. "And now he gives it to others," she said.

Although he is a Catholic, Andrea Bocelli describes his faith in what are perhaps broader terms. "I am philosophically a believer," he said. "I've never, not for one moment, believed in coincidences. I've always thought with a strange certainty that the world is a manifestation of an evident intelligence. This is my belief." He attends Mass and other church functions with his young family in his wife's hometown of Pontedera, but he doesn't consider himself a devout Catholic in the strictest sense of the term. "I am certainly a believer, but my belonging to a religion arises mostly from the fact that my family is Catholic. I am surely not a 'good' Catholic!" he said.

Andrea's warm and thoughtful personality is in harmony with the character of rural Tuscany, where he has always lived. Whenever he travels, even if his family is with him, he anxiously looks forward to returning to La Sterza or his home on the Tuscan coast. Because celebrity came to him later in life, he doesn't fear that it will corrupt him or shake him from the serene core that his family, his spirituality, and his relationship with nature have given him. His parents were not ostentatious about their wealth, and Andrea has inherited this attitude toward money. "I have grown up in wealth and at the same time in a temperate family. I have not missed anything, but I've learned to live with measure," he said. "I came to realize already as an adolescent that I was deep down very fortunate. I had many things. I had affection and health, thank God. I consider myself fortunate."

When Andrea returns home from a tour or concert or recording session, he loves to settle into the quiet life of La Sterza and Lajatico. He goes to the tiny café on the Lajatico town square to sit with his brother Alberto, drink espresso, or play a game of chess. He strolls through the familiar streets and stops to chat with old friends. Andrea feels deeply connected to this place and these people. "I am among them, and I conserve with all my strength those roots that are part of my Tuscan heritage and part of these people," he said.

Lajatico's history includes one other famous native son, Gillo Dorfles. The painter is one of Italy's most distinguished artists and currently a teacher at the Brera Academy of Fine Arts in Milan and art critic for *Corriere della Sera*. Lajatico's two famous offspring are both men of the arts who have made their small community extremely proud.

Speaking of Bocelli, mayor Stefano Paperini said, "Currently there is a lot of admira-

Photos: Susan Turner

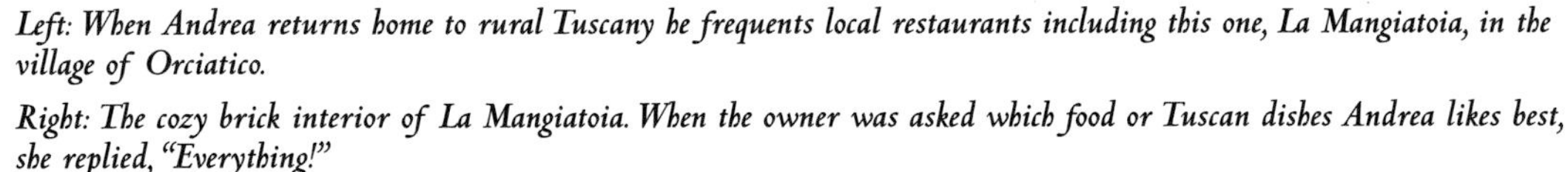

Left: When Andrea returns home to rural Tuscany he frequents local restaurants including this one, La Mangiatoia, in the village of Orciatico.

Right: The cozy brick interior of La Mangiatoia. When the owner was asked which food or Tuscan dishes Andrea likes best, she replied, "Everything!"

tion. Even though everybody believed in Andrea, for him to explode like he has is amazing. Maybe it took Andrea longer than it should have to make it big, considering his talent. He's still young, but he could have made it sooner. The people here have always admired his voice; currently they not only admire him but they are also very proud of him. He's from here, from this land, and they are pleased that he is so successful. In fact, when Andrea comes into Lajatico, in the piazza, he goes around undisturbed. He has his coffee, nobody bothers him."

Paperini has observed that his friend is a bit self-conscious because of his fame and doesn't want to attract any special attention to himself in town. "There's some shyness now," he continued. "He's become a very famous person." No longer just a neighbor or friend, Andrea has become a world-famous artist who belongs to the world, and everyone in his hometown looks at him differently. "The Andrea from five years ago is gone, he doesn't exist anymore," said Paperini. "There is a lot of admiration and respect for what he's doing. We are all happy for the success he's had. He comes back here frequently and appreciates what we do."

Part of this appreciation is for the local cuisine. La Mangiatoia, a restaurant in the nearby village of Orciatico, has been serving Andrea local specialties for years. The owners, Paolo and Lorella Vannucci, say that he likes "everything," but some of the dishes that came to mind were *panzanella,* a salad made with crumbled Tuscan bread, fresh vegetables, and olive oil; *zuppa di cavolo,* a thick cabbage soup; *rigatino al forno,* a baked pasta dish; and *pappardelle cinghiale,* a dish made with wild boar. Andrea's sister-in-law, Vania Cenzatti, adds that he is crazy about a very simple dish, *pasta al burro,* noodles with butter. One of the regional specialties that Andrea does not indulge in is wine, even though he enjoys it. "Singers must follow strict diets like athletes," he said. "The problem with my success is that it forbids me to drink Chianti with lasagna or spaghetti."

Like other neighboring villages, Orciatico is becoming a popular site for Tuscan *agriturismo,* agricultural or country tourism. Rather than taking an Italian holiday in a bustling, tourist-filled city, travelers are discovering the joys of renting a room or house in a small village or on one of the surrounding farms. Tuscany's remote farming communities are keenly aware that the local scenery, quiet recreation, marvelous food and Chianti, and friendly people are irresistible to overworked and overstimulated Europeans and Americans.

For Andrea, coming home to La Sterza also means returning to the horse trails he has ridden most of his life. "In the village where I live, I marked out a more or less fixed area," said Andrea. "This one I know very well—every slope, every way, every tree is familiar to me."

Luciano Pavarotti, Andrea's most famous friend and countryman, shares his passion for horses. Over the years Pavarotti's equestrian obsession has resulted in a large stable of thoroughbreds on his estate in Modena and the creation of the Pavarotti International Horse Show, an annual event complete with concert. Like Andrea, Luciano has loved horses since he was a boy. "I see my love of artistry and beauty and my love of sports coming together in horses," the tenor writes in *Pavarotti: My World*. "Just to watch these animals gives me great pleasure. For me it is something incredibly beautiful to watch one of these magnificent creatures go over a jump. If he is good, he looks ahead and gauges his distance and figures out what he has to do. It's very much like a tenor when he knows that the high notes are coming. We must think ahead, test our power, and focus our energies on the obstacle that we must get beyond."

Andrea admits, "The only true luxury I allow myself are my horses." The demands of the singer's career take him away from his country home for long periods of time, however,

Andrea's home in La Sterza. The singer describes this countryside as a place filled with "beautiful nature, history, and simple and honest people." It is, he says, "the place where I was born and spend my most truly relaxing times."

Photo: Susan Turner

and in the late 1990s he sold all but one of his horses, Gisele, because he felt he could not give each of them the attention they deserved. The lessons Andrea Bocelli has learned on the back of a horse are alive in everything he does. "The first thing that counts in my life was my encounter with music," he said. "It was my first medicine: it calmed me if I was irritable, it made me feel peaceful. The second important thing was my passion for animals—above all, horses. I would be very excited by the idea of riding a difficult horse, just as I would feel similarly excited when I started to sing—to approach a very difficult piece of music. One of the reasons behind my success is this tenacity, which has been there forever, this refusal to accept defeat."

Andrea went to the university in Pisa, birthplace of Galileo and home of the famous Leaning Tower.

Photo: Susan Turner

2
"My Way"

The Bocellis are practical people. Sandro and Edi always respected and supported Andrea's musical talent, but they also valued the security that a professional trade or vocation would give each of their two sons. "In the countryside where I grew up," said Andrea, "they didn't think it was possible to be happy singing. My parents wanted me to have a serious education, with real professional opportunities. . . . They said I could try to sing but they reminded me that people cannot live just with their dreams. You must have something more concrete." Andrea understands that World War II was partly responsible for his parents' attitude. "I experienced childhood at the end of the fifties and at the beginning of the sixties," he said, "a good decade after the war. There was still much misery and need. Therefore my upbringing was strict, the values concrete. . . . One appreciated small things." Like his parents, Andrea felt that music was not the most practical choice if he wanted to have a prosperous future. "I wanted to learn a civil job," he recalled. "Love for the art does not guarantee a proper income."

During his last year in high school, which he attended in Pontedera, Andrea considered which profession he would most like to pursue. There were lawyers scattered throughout the Bocelli family tree, and Andrea's parents encouraged this choice. Although his high school grades hadn't been outstanding, Andrea did well in the final exam and realized that his academic potential was quite good. Before graduation he had been torn between pursuing music and law, but "then I got my diploma, with full marks," he explained. "It was a surprise, because I did not do that well in school but I got a good grade on my final exam, and this was a temptation. At that point I decided to follow the course that some family members before me had taken, the course of law; also, there was maybe a tacit request and pressure from my family."

Photo: Susan Turner

Andrea's university was a short walk from the Leaning Tower, which began to list in 1274 before the building was even finished.

Andrea enrolled in the nearby University of Pisa, one of the most prestigious schools in Italy and an important center of learning and science in Europe since the Middle Ages. Just north of the Arno River on Via Sapienza (Wisdom

This page: The law school at Pisa. Law has been studied here since the twelfth century, when Pisa became a center of learning that drew students from all over Europe.
Facing page: The law school of the Università degli Studii in Pisa where Andrea earned a law degree.

Photos: Susan Turner

Street), the Università degli Studii building was built in the 1400s—with additions made in every century thereafter. Even older than the university's buildings is the institution itself, which was a center for teaching law in the twelfth century and medicine in the thirteenth century. The university's most famous pupil was Galileo Galilei (1564–1642), a native of Pisa who entered the university at the age of seventeen and became a lecturer of mathematics there at the age of twenty-five. During his three-year teaching post he conducted some of his most famous experiments, including dropping balls off the roof of the Leaning Tower to study the acceleration of falling bodies. Galileo's discovery of the laws of gravity and the oscillations of a pendulum (forerunner to the invention of the clock) were all based on research he did in Pisa. His pendulums can be found throughout the city, including one that hangs from the ceiling in the cathedral.

Roughly half of Pisa's buildings were destroyed by Allied bombing raids during World War II, and the Leaning Tower and cathedral were spared only by a matter of a few yards. Pisa is situated on the north and south banks of the Arno River, about seven miles (11 kilometers) from where the river flows into the Mediterranean Sea. The first human beings settled along these banks during the Bronze Age. Pisa became a Roman colony in the third century B.C. and a vital seaport under Imperial Rome. In the Middle Ages Pisa thrived as a major trading port and became the wealthy center of radical new advances in science and architecture. With a vast merchant fleet and navy that defended the west coast, Pisa was one of the port cities that controlled the seas around Italy.

Modern Pisa may be one of Italy's most popular tourist spots, but it's even more renowned as a university town. Of the ninety-seven thousand people who

ANDREA'S FOUR YEARS AS A UNIVERSITY STUDENT WERE A STEADY MIX OF MUSIC AND STUDY. EVEN THOUGH HE WAS SERIOUSLY ON COURSE TO BECOME A LAWYER, HE FOUND A WAY TO BLEND MUSIC WITH HIS SOCIAL LIFE.

live in the city, forty thousand are students at the university. The small streets around the law school Andrea attended, which were designed for thirteenth-century foot traffic, are a constant snarl of cars, city buses, pedestrians, and motorcycles that perilously scoot through the smallest spaces. Students have a choice between two types of university programs, the *laurea breve* (short degree) and the *laurea*. The shorter program takes from two to three years. The *laurea* degree takes from four to six years and requires a dissertation. Andrea's course in *giurisprudenza* (law) was a four-year *laurea* degree program. The courses included the history of Roman and medieval law, ecclesiastical law, comparative judicial systems, law of the European community, parliamentary law, and political economics. Andrea delved into the subject matter and enjoyed it. "To this day I do not regret it because I did it also with a passion," he said. "In fact, I won a prize in jurisprudence." With the help of a braille computer and translation software, Andrea never missed a lecture and could study all the materials like everyone else. "The computer was an indispensable help," he said. "With the computer my lectures were transformed into braille and thus I could study." For his dissertation project Andrea chose to write about the French Enlightenment thinker Charles de Montesquieu (1689–1755), the political philosopher whose ideas about a nonmonarchical government greatly influenced other leaders in his time, including those who drafted the U.S. constitution.

Andrea's four years as a university student were a steady mix of music and study. Even though he was seriously on course to become a lawyer, he found a way to blend music with his social life. Hanging out with friends a night or two each week in piano bars, Andrea began to sit at the keyboard himself and play pop standards. He became so popular that he was asked to appear regularly, and soon he had a steady flow of income from making music. When exams approached he took time off and spent every evening studying, but during the rest of the academic year his job and social life revolved around the local piano bars. During the first few months he didn't sing, but only played the piano. Andrea hadn't sung much in public, and singing for friends is often more nerve-wracking than performing for strangers. Recalling these first jobs, Bocelli said that he spent the evenings playing piano but "never singing at first because I was too scared." Even though he hadn't listened to very much popular music, he was impressed by how musically interesting some of the classic songs were, such as those of Frank Sinatra and the French singers Charles Aznavour, Jacques Brel, and Edith Piaf. "To be sincere about it I will admit that when I was doing the piano bar work I was very interested in the artistic aspects of it all, and very often I would perform the . . . typical piano bar fare," he said. "I thought then that it wasn't so bad and I quite enjoyed singing those songs—but my heart was always with classical music." He spent quality time learning the English words to American pop songs by Whitney Houston and Stevie Wonder, which were very popular with the lounge crowd. One of the staples of his English-language song list was Sinatra's signature piece, "My Way," which Andrea would later dust off and sing in front of President Bill Clinton. Another favorite song, sung in French, was Charles Aznavour's "La Bohème," a sentimental waltz tune with words by Jacques Plante that reminisce about the glory days of being young, poor, and full of great expectations. While singing the second verse of this song, which speaks of sitting in cafés and imagining future fame, Andrea may have been thinking about his own dreams of making a life in music—and his determination to turn them into reality:

Nous ne cessions d'y croire . . .

We never stopped believing . . .

Bocelli also loved to play and sing pieces by the legendary Italian singer/songwriter Francesco Guccini, the artist who inspired him to write his own songs when he was a student in Bologna. Guccini, who has recorded twenty albums since 1967 and is constantly on tour in Italy, was a major inspiration to Bocelli. "Guccini was a significant parenthesis in my life," he said. "It was in the years of the youth movement in the seventies. Guccini was sung by everyone! I was touched by his lyrics. The art of writing, of composing verses . . . goes beyond everything. I was so infected with this and with his personality that I sought to do it as well."

Sitting behind the piano and playing popular love songs was a perfect way to meet girls. Young women found Andrea's finesse at the piano, romantic voice, and sexy good

Andrea and Enrica. "I fell in love with him when I heard him sing," said Enrica.

looks irresistible. Bocelli admits to being fortunate in the romance department. He made a fabulous impression on young women and never lacked for dates. One evening a seventeen-year-old young woman named Enrica introduced herself between numbers and made quite an impression on him.

Enrica found Andrea at a club called Boschetto (the Grove) in Chianni, a small town west of Lajatico. Chianni is set on a 932-foot hill that offers a wonderful view of the countryside and a tall, rolling set of hills to the south called the Poggio Biancanelle. The curvy, tree-lined road leading up to Chianni turns in to the narrow main street in the center of town. Boschetto, which has since closed, was an outdoor lounge where friends could have drinks and listen to music under the stars. Andrea Bocelli had earned his law degree by this time, but continued to perform in the piano lounges to earn money.

Remembering the first night they met, Andrea said, "Enrica asked me whether I wanted to have a drink with her. I was always rather successful with girls, but I considered Enrica as someone special, precisely for her naturalness. From the first moment it went pleasantly between us. We haven't let go of each

Photo: Susan Turner

Photo © Franco Silvi

Top: Andrea and Enrica met in a piano bar in the town of Chianni, where Andrea was singing popular songs of Frank Sinatra and French singers Charles Aznavour and Jacques Brel. The open-air bar was a popular spot for young people to meet and enjoy summer evenings under the stars.

Bottom: The couple at home. Andrea and Enrica were married in her home town of Pontedera in June, 1992. "Apart from my mother," Andrea said, "Enrica is the only person in whom I have total confidence. She is, with my horses, my first public. She was the first to hear 'Con te partirò,' and also the first to cry upon listening to it. I knew it would be a success."

other ever since."

Enrica Cenzatti was born in 1971 in Pontedera, a town of about twenty-six thousand people that lies between Lajatico and Pisa. Both she and her sister, Vania, are outgoing, smart, petite, and attractive, with long black hair and dark brown eyes. Unlike Andrea, Enrica loved rock and pop music while she was growing up. Her father, a lawyer, listened to classical music at home, but she wasn't interested in it. "Our house was full of classical music because our father loved it," said Vania. However, Enrica's favorite singer was a rock star from Minneapolis, Minnesota. "Enrica loved Prince," said her sister. "She listened to rock, for better or worse, just like everyone else her age. I believe she has all of Prince's records; they weren't on CD yet."

One summer night Enrica came home from Chianni, where she had just met Andrea for the first time. The girls' parents were away, and Enrica came home late and rushed to her sister's room. "I remember I was in bed one night," Vania said, "and she woke me up. I was still half asleep when she shook me by the shoulders and started telling me she had met someone she liked. 'He's so handsome! So handsome!' she yelled at me."

Andrea had felt the same strong attraction that first night. "When she touched my hand, it was love that hit me. I knew I had just met the love of my life," he said. "I noticed she was a very spontaneous, natural, honest person. She was very young, very sweet-natured. It was very easy for her to captivate me." Enrica knew that she had found her true love the first time she heard Andrea perform at the piano. "I fell in love with him when I heard him sing Jacques Brel's 'Amsterdam' and Aznavour's 'La Bohème,' " she said.

"Tears filled my eyes. His voice expressed such sweetness, kindness, and generosity which no woman could resist. With the passing years I have come to understand that the man is equal to his voice." Every evening Andrea tossed a few arias into his mix of Italian, English, and French standards at Boschetto. Enrica was very fond of "Non piangere, Liù," a tenor aria from Puccini's *Turandot*, and it became "their" song.

Enrica returned to Boschetto several times after that first night and had many conversations with Andrea. Eventually he asked her out to dinner, and they had more time to tell their life stories. "We spoke of many things," recalled Andrea, "where we came from, writers and singers we liked." They discovered that they were both voracious readers and shared a love of French literature. As they became more comfortable with each other, Enrica asked about Andrea's blindness. He told her about his inherited glaucoma and the soccer accident that took his sight at age twelve. Enrica had already observed how unself-conscious Andrea was about his blindness, and in that conversation she learned everything about the attitude he had had toward it since childhood. He told her that on earth there are "lean, fat, small, and tall persons, those who see and the others [who don't]. Anyway, a man who can talk to animals and can go horseback riding is

"HIS VOICE EXPRESSED SUCH SWEETNESS, KINDNESS, AND GENEROSITY WHICH NO WOMAN COULD RESIST," ENRICA SAID. "WITH THE PASSING YEARS I HAVE COME TO UNDERSTAND THAT THE MAN IS EQUAL TO HIS VOICE."

Enrica, Andrea, and Amos taking a stroll in Pontedera, Enrica's hometown.

not and never will be disabled." Enrica realized that "for him, it is an immutable situation, a 'joke from nature.' It was the only time we talked about it."

On June 27, 1992, four years after they met, Andrea and Enrica were married at the San Leonardo church in Lajatico. After the wedding everyone drove down to Edi and Sandro Bocelli's house in La Sterza for an elaborate outdoor reception. For their honeymoon the couple took a cruise in the Mediterranean.

Enrica and Andrea are rarely apart, and Andrea calls her "the guide of my life, figuratively and literally." "I always need someone to accompany me," he said [Andrea has never used a white cane], "and just because of that she plays an irreplaceable role in my life. When we go on tour abroad, she comes along as many time as possible and then she tells me everything—what there is to see around us. This is no burden for her; she is a lovely narrator and she knows how to describe picturesquely." Andrea also relies upon Enrica's sensitivity to his music and singing. "Apart from my mother," he said, "she is the only person in whom I have total confidence. She is, with my horses, my first public. She was the first to hear "Con te partirò," and also the first to cry upon listening to it. I knew it would be a success."

Andrea and Enrica are cheerful, witty, energetic people who complement each other well. "I am convinced," said Andrea, "that everyone has a match on earth. I let my instinct guide me. To me, Enrica is the most beautiful and the most extraordinary of all women."

Enrica Bocelli described her husband as "neither a sad person nor a tortured one."

She said, "He belongs to the category of the whimsical, inventing life day after day. He is gifted for happiness. And not everybody possesses that talent." Being Andrea's guide has become completely second-nature to Enrica. "I forget entirely that he is blind," she said. "I only notice it in a few situations, for example, if we're out and I have to drive the car back home, though I am very tired. We live as if he could see."

After graduating from the university, Andrea had taken a job as a public defender at the Palazzo di Giustizia (courthouse) in Pisa. The courthouse was built in 1958 and stands in drab contrast to the medieval and Renaissance treasures for which the town is famous. Just a few steps away on the Via Palestro, however, is the exquisite Teatro Verdi, where Andrea would later make his first appearance in an opera.

Photo: Susan Turner

After graduating from law school, Andrea took a job as a public defender at the Palazzo di Giustizia in Pisa. He was fascinated with law and liked his work, but was glad that his clients "had committed only small offenses." After working at the courthouse for one year, he made the life-changing decision to quit and devote himself to a career in music.

Andrea was not yet married when he took the job in the public defender's office. Taking the cases of people in the community who couldn't afford or obtain legal assistance, Andrea liked his work. Fortunately, he says, "my clients had committed only small offenses." He admits that his most memorable case wasn't a brilliant defense for one of the department's clients—but for himself. "I had to fight the tax authorities, who had seized part of my assets because they were misinformed on my income," he explains. The assets in question were his musical instruments: guitars, a flute and a saxophone, and other prized instruments he had collected over the years. Andrea enjoyed the work but he couldn't take his mind off music. "I considered law fascinating," he says, "but I was gripped much more by music. . . . The problem was that inside of me I lived in a world of sounds." Finally, after one year on the job, he made a life-changing decision. He would quit the public defender's office and give his singing a chance. Instead of being pushed to the side, his world of sounds now moved to center stage.

Since childhood Andrea had sensed that his destiny lay in singing. At this point in his life, he felt compelled to act on his instinct and not ignore the call any longer. Such a call can feel stronger than any other force in one's life and speak more loudly than personal wishes or family pressures. In the words of psychiatrist Carl Jung, the call to be an artist "is a kind of innate drive that seizes a human being and makes him its instrument. The artist is not a person endowed with free will who seeks his own ends, but one who allows art to realize its purposes through him." Andrea had always felt that the decision to become a singer was out of his hands and determined by others. "I don't think one really decides to be a singer," he said. "Other people decide it for you by their reaction." Since he first stood on his little kitchen stage and sang for his relatives, the positive response of others has given Bocelli the motivation to perform. The decision to leave the law and pursue a career in music grew out of his sense of responsibility to develop the God-given talent that gave him so much pleasure and seemed to please others, too.

After leaving the public defender's office, Andrea sometimes worried about his future and felt frustrated that his singing career wasn't going anywhere. He was torn between his confidence in himself and his parents' concerns over his future. To help him sort out his feelings and express them to his family, he wrote a poem to his father. "It is a poem that I wrote in a very delicate moment in my life when I was not able to attain any results and my parents were worried," he said. In a few lines of the song, Andrea tries to convince his father that the road he has chosen will not destroy him, even if it is a choice his father cannot understand: *Nothing in the world will make me forget that I can win.*

Andrea would later commission a songwriter to set this poem to music, and he recorded the song, "A mio padre" on his album *Sogno.*

Even though he didn't stay with his law career, Andrea Bocelli doesn't regret a moment of his laureate education or his legal work. He has always jumped completely into things that interest him, including studying literature and law. His education and legal experience also give him an edge in dealing with the music industry of the 1990s. "From time to time in my job now it's also good to know about the law," he told a reporter with a laugh.

When Enrica met Andrea he had already been through his short stint as a lawyer. He

Enrica Bocelli on the beach in the summer of 1997 with her son Amos and pregnant with her second son, who would be born that October.

Photo © Franco Silvi

had returned to the piano bars to finance his new education: voice and piano lessons. After they were married, Enrica left in the mornings to work in the silver shop she still owns with her sister in Pontedera. The small, charming shop sells jewelry, clocks, silver picture frames, and other articles. Andrea practiced piano and singing during the day and went to work in the piano bars a few evenings a week.

At the beginning of their relationship Andrea was an unknown lounge singer with only dreams of making a career in music. The success that quickly followed his first appearance at the San Remo Festival was something that neither of them expected. Enrica's sister recalled that the couple had talked about Andrea's dreams of success but were not prepared for what actually happened. "They wished it because more or less Andrea's desire was to be able to support his family by singing," she said. "So he tried to make it his profession, his job, not simply a hobby. But they never dreamed of it happening at this level. It's become so much grander than they could have imagined."

Three years after their wedding Andrea and Enrica had their first child, Amos. Born February 22, 1995, their son was named after one of Andrea's dearest, oldest friends from Lajatico. From the beginning of their marriage, the couple had had long discussions about starting a family. "My wife wanted a little family very much," said Andrea, "and so did I, but I didn't want my children to have to go through life blind, just like me. Therefore, we asked several specialists for advice. Every specialist reassured us. The chance that our baby would be born with an eye abnormality was as small as if I had been born without this eye disease. When my wife was pregnant the first time . . . I prayed for a healthy child each day. And I am glad that God heard my prayers."

When Enrica went into labor with Amos, Andrea was on the Italian Riviera near the French border performing in the San Remo Festival. He regretted that he couldn't be there. "Enrica gave birth to him all alone," he said. "I thought it was terrible, but I couldn't do otherwise. I had been asked to present myself at the famous San Remo Festival, which finally became my big break. Just before I began to get ready, I got a phone call that

This page: Enrica and Andrea Bocelli out and about in the summer of 1997. Enrica is expecting her second child.

Facing page: In October, 1997, Andrea nervously waits on the terrace of the Lotti Hospital in Pontedera while Enrica is in the delivery room. He hired an elite group of security professionals to keep the press and photographers away from the hospital.

Photos © Franco Silvi

I had become a father. I could have cried with happiness." This was Andrea's first appearance at the main San Remo event, following his win in the preliminary competition the year before. By the time Enrica became pregnant again, Andrea had become a star with a full schedule of concerts around the world, but he blocked off October and November of 1997 to be with her when she would deliver. On October 8 of that year the Bocellis' second son, Matteo, was born. "This time I didn't want to miss the birth of my child," he said.

Andrea was the picture of the nervous father while Enrica was in labor with Matteo.

Pacing back and forth on a terrace of the Lotti Hospital in Pontedera, he couldn't bear to experience his wife in pain. "It is difficult and sad to witness suffering," he said. "The joy to know that something wonderful is happening is not enough. This is why I did not have the courage to stay with Enrica in the delivery room. I had to wait outside nervously." To insure the privacy of his wife and himself while Enrica was in the hospital, Andrea hired five security specialists from an international security company called La First. They sealed off the clinic to everyone except staff and close family members of the other patients, with Bocelli's elite guard standing watch at the exits and outside Enrica's room.

With her mother, Giuliana, at her side, Enrica gave birth to Matteo at one-thirty that afternoon. The local newspaper carried the news in blissful detail:

> With a labor that lasted about three hours, she gave birth to a splendid boy, the second in Bocelli's house. The child, wearing a little shirt in white and pink (which brings good fortune) has been transferred to the loving arms of the mother, who in the afternoon has started to breastfeed him. The labor was quick, to such an extent that the family of the new mother was not prepared. In the next days the family will come back to the new house at Forte dei Marmi. Matteo will find a new little room completely for himself. The furnishings have been chosen during the nine months of sweet waiting by Enrica.

Just as he had done with Amos, Andrea held the newborn Matteo in his arms immediately after he was born. "I was overcome with happiness, love and tenderness. . . . Right after he was washed, I studied him with my hands: his downy little head, his little nose, everything on the tiny body," he recalled. Andrea explained that he sees his chil-

dren with his hands. "As I once could see for some years, after, I know what most things look like," he said. "If I don't know it, then I feel it with my hands. I always say that I look with my hands. I know precisely how Amos looks, and I also know the looks of my second son. How I can see with my hands I can't explain." Andrea and Enrica had shopped for baby furniture together during the last two months of her pregnancy with Matteo, something which he found very touching and enjoyable.

Before they left the hospital in Pontedera, Andrea gave Enrica a gift. "The singer, to commemorate the happy event," wrote the Pontedera newspaper, "has presented his wife with a Reverso watch in steel and gold of a value of about eight million lire [$4,400]. Enrica is a passionate collector of watches and had expressed the desire to have one as a gift."

"There is nothing that makes me happier than being a father," Andrea said. His family is "my reason for living, my drug, my oxygen. I feel I need them more than they need me. . . . These children represent everything to me. I want to surpass myself so they will be proud of me, so that they can carry the torch, whatever career they choose. I want to be an example, a model and a guiding light for them."

Andrea is not a parent who lavishes his children with gifts or creates a home that is full of luxury. Like Sandro and Edi, he is happy to keep his lifestyle very comfortable, but not showy. "I rarely bring gifts along when returning home from a journey," he said. "A dad who always comes home with a lot of souvenirs oversaturates them too much. I am of

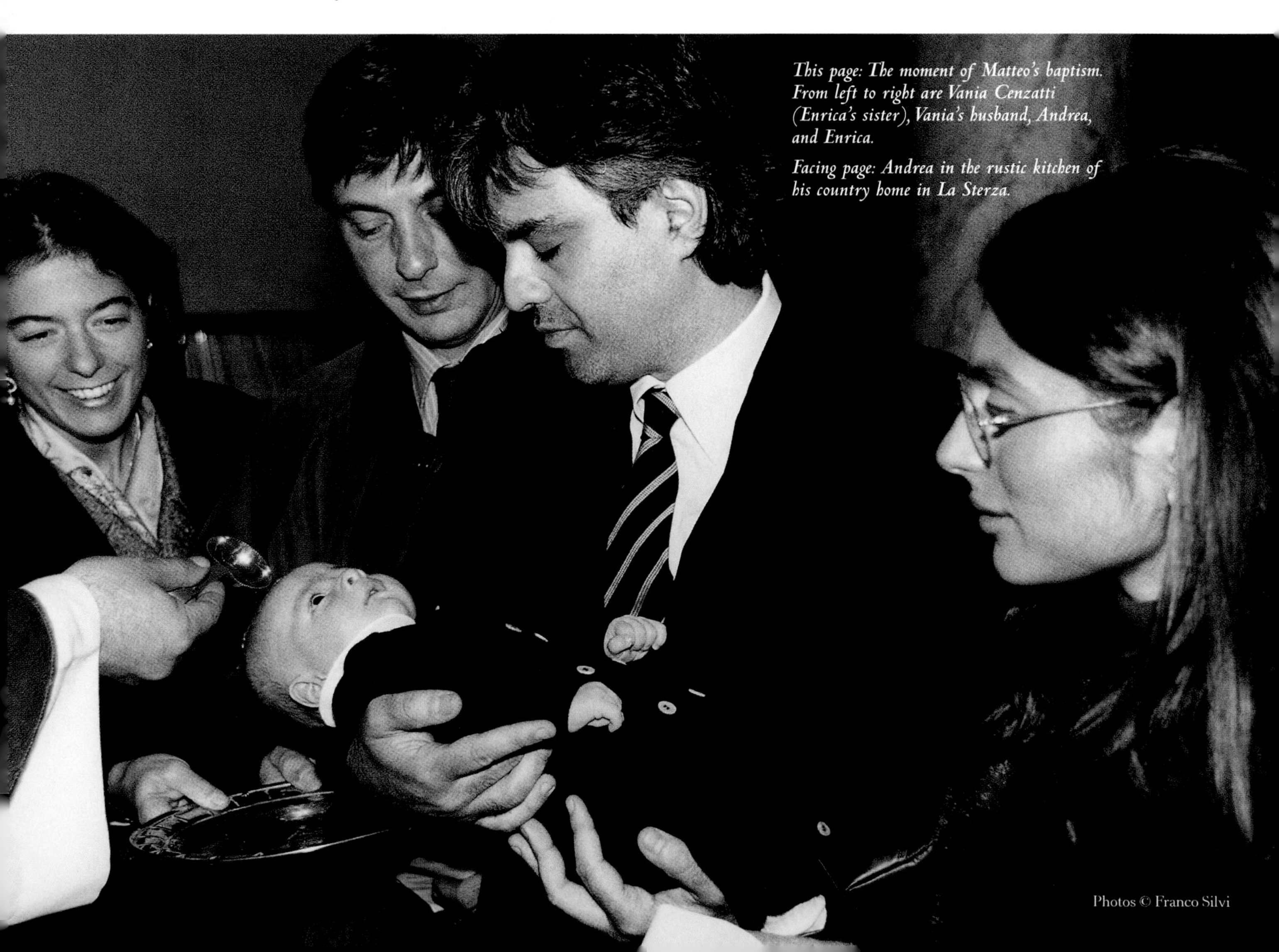

This page: The moment of Matteo's baptism. From left to right are Vania Cenzatti (Enrica's sister), Vania's husband, Andrea, and Enrica.

Facing page: Andrea in the rustic kitchen of his country home in La Sterza.

the opinion that one has to desire gifts, to dream of them, to wait for them; only in this way can one appreciate them. In short, my wife is the one who often buys gifts, while I try to explain to my sons how useless they are."

Amos and Matteo have black hair and beautiful dark eyes. Enrica described the differences in personality between the two boys: "Amos looks more like Andrea and he's very serious, doesn't laugh or smile very often. Matteo is closer to me: happier, smilier, more radiant."

In the same spirit as his parents, Andrea hopes to give his children every opportunity to explore their interests and pursue whatever occupation they desire. His own parents did this for him and Alberto, and Andrea recognizes that "in this aspect we are both very fortunate. We had the space, the liberty to determine our choice, to decide that which is just for the young to decide." He hopes to pass along to his children his positive attitude and deep-seated sense that anything is possible. "I will try to set an example for them of optimism and belief in the future. In the end, they must discover life for them-

This page: Andrea and his firstborn son, Amos, who was named after one of Andrea's dearest friends from Lajatico.

Facing page: Andrea singing during Matteo's baptism service.

This page: The family gathers in front of the Christmas tree for a family portrait in 1997. When Andrea travels on long concert tours he brings the family along, but on short trips or when one of the children is ill he travels without them, regretfully. To Andrea, his family is "my reason for living, my drug, my oxygen." He says, "I feel I need them more than they need me."

Facing page: Amos, Andrea, and Enrica on the patio of their seaside home in Forte dei Marmi.

selves." Andrea is the product of an affectionate and close family and is creating the same qualities in his own. "In my family, our affection has always been very solid," he said. "As a father, I always try to recreate for my children the way that I was raised, and always hold present two principles in which I believe: optimism and faith, trust in others. He who does not have faith in others will receive mistrust in return."

Andrea Bocelli's biggest priority is his family, and he revealed this during his extensive American tours in 1998 and early 1999. In order to give his sons the best opportunity to see the United States, he chose to travel by bus rather than use the chartered jets whenever time permitted. Ana Maria Martinez, the soprano who shared the stage with him during the tours, recalled that "he always put his family first; his children are first for him. If the schedule didn't permit time for leisurely travel, they'd get on the bus that night, instead of sleep at the hotel and be comfortable like the rest of us, and start off so their children could see things during the ride the next morning. He explained to me that 'they won't really be able to see it if we're flying, and I want them to actually see the land.' "

In the months that the Bocellis were expecting their second child they bought a house on the Tuscany coast in Forte dei Marmi. Andrea had begun to suffer from allergies in the country, and felt that the climate by the sea was much healthier for his voice. They kept the house in La Sterza and divide their time between the two homes. Forte dei Marmi is one of a string of luxurious resort towns along the coastline just north of Pisa. The magnificent Apuan Alps also follow the coast, giving Forte dei Marmi the double beauty of mountains and sea. The town is filled with boutiques and fine restaurants, and the seashore is lined with beach clubs

Photo: Susan Turner

Photo © Franco Silvi

that charge a fee for lying on a "sunning table" or sitting on a canvas chair beneath an umbrella. From the water, each club can be identified by the color of the umbrellas and chairs that form neat, precise rows in the sand.

The Bocelli house sits on the main coastline road directly across from a cluster of beach clubs. Before the start of the busy summer season, the road and the neighborhood are quiet, but from July through September there is a constant flow of traffic. Surrounding Andrea's yard along the road is a tall, dark green plastic mesh fence that many homeowners in the area use for privacy. The entry to the house, which is called Il Balzo (the Bounce or Leap), is a tiny lane off the main road lined with thick trees, from which come the pleasant sounds of mourning doves and other birds. Inside

Photos: Susan Turner

This page, top: The front of the Bocellis' house on the sea is protected by a dark green plastic mesh fence for privacy.

This page, bottom: One of the beach views at Forte dei Marmi. After the birth of their first son, the Bocellis bought a second home in this fashionable resort town on the Tuscany coast.

Facing page, top: A marker on Andrea's house in Forte dei Marmi displays the name of the house, Il Balzo.

Facing page, bottom: Andrea strikes a pose on his patio at Forte dei Marmi.

the fence is a pretty landscaped yard dotted with children's toys, including a colorful plastic playhouse. Brick arches rise over the patio leading into the house, and wooden shutters on the windows keep out the early summer heat.

"This house was a bargain," Andrea said. "If I made a few renovations, it was only to keep it in shape, nothing more." In early 1999 Andrea and Enrica also bought an apartment in Monte Carlo on the French Riviera. They like the idea of Amos and Matteo growing up with French and English as well as Italian. But Forte dei Marmi is still one of Andrea's favorite retreats from the world, second only to the riding paths of La Sterza. At home with his family, Andrea spends a lot of time in the kitchen cooking pasta or making a huge salad according to an old family recipe. "I am unequaled for salad

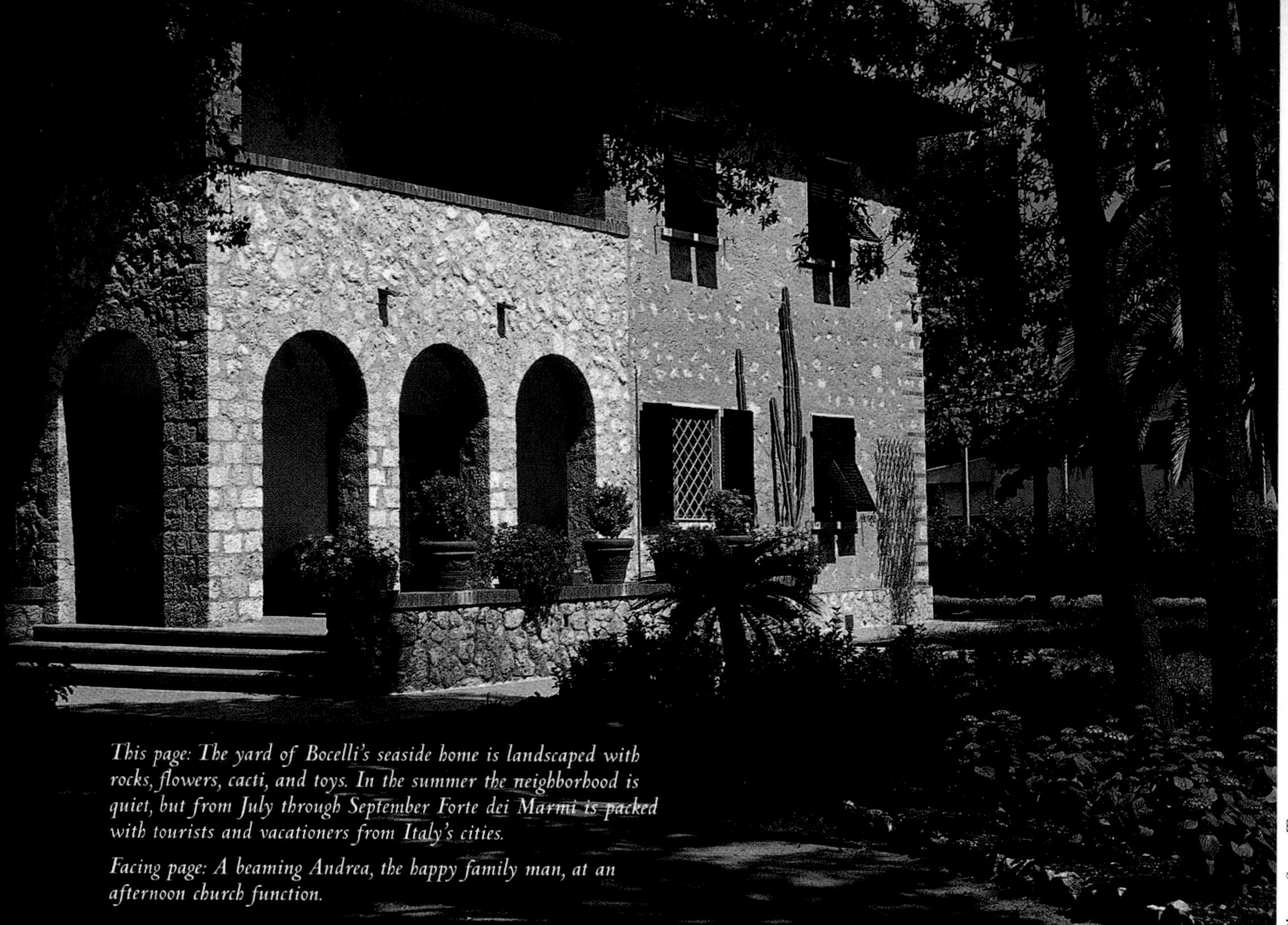

This page: The yard of Bocelli's seaside home is landscaped with rocks, flowers, cacti, and toys. In the summer the neighborhood is quiet, but from July through September Forte dei Marmi is packed with tourists and vacationers from Italy's cities.

Facing page: A beaming Andrea, the happy family man, at an afternoon church function.

Photo: Susan Turner

dressings," he said. "It is a secret my mother transmitted to me." He hugs and plays with his sons, sings to his wife, listens to music, and is a very contented man. The house is comfortable and roomy, but one day the Bocelli family may have to find a bigger villa in the town.

"First I was very anxious about the idea of becoming a father," Andrea said, "but since I've had my two sons I'd like to have eleven of them. A little team."

Photo © Franco Silvi

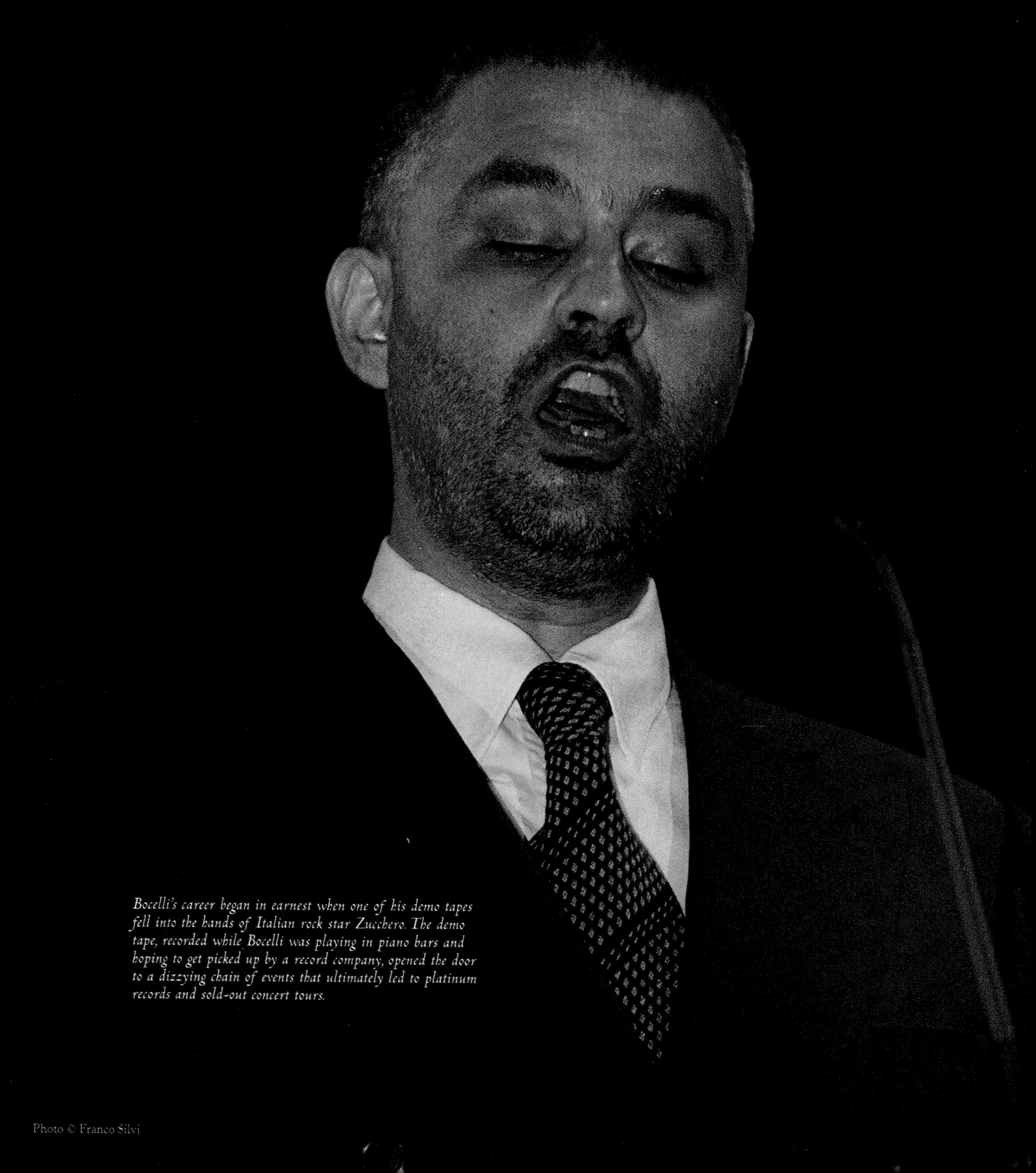

Bocelli's career began in earnest when one of his demo tapes fell into the hands of Italian rock star Zucchero. The demo tape, recorded while Bocelli was playing in piano bars and hoping to get picked up by a record company, opened the door to a dizzying chain of events that ultimately led to platinum records and sold-out concert tours.

Photo © Franco Silvi

The Calm Sea of Victory
3

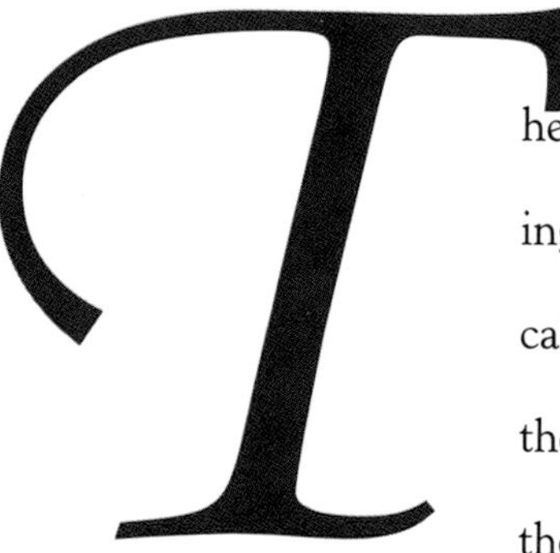

he phone call woke Andrea up. "This is Maestro Pavarotti speaking," said the voice. Still half asleep, Andrea thought it was a prank call, but held back from hanging up. "This is Maestro Pavarotti," the caller repeated. "Then," said Andrea, "coming to, I recognized the voice."

Pavarotti was calling to invite Bocelli to sing on his upcoming "Pavarotti and Friends" concert in Modena. It was the follow-up call of Bocelli's dreams, for he had not met the world's most famous tenor but had received a career-making endorsement from him. It had all started with a run-of-the-mill demo tape sent out to record companies by the unknown piano bar singer from Pisa. The story of Andrea Bocelli's overnight success could be called "The Tale of the Tape."

During his long and frustrating foray into lounge music, Andrea recorded demo tapes that he felt represented his best popular songs and arias. He sent them to record companies and recording studio executives, never giving up the hope that someday, someone would show an interest and offer him a record contract. One day, out of the blue, his persistence paid off.

In 1992 Italian rock star Zucchero ("Sugar," a.k.a. Adelmo Fornaciari) needed a tenor to record his own important demo tape project. He had written a duet entitled "Miserere" with Bono of U2 and wanted to interest Luciano Pavarotti in recording it with him. To give the song its full effect—the contrast between Zucchero's gravelly voice and that of a classical singer—he wanted to record the demo tape with an operatic tenor. One of the engineers in the recording studio recalled a demo tape, sent in by an Italian tenor, that included some arias. They listened to it and put Bocelli on the list to come in and audition.

Zucchero was astounded by what he heard when Bocelli came to the mike. His voice had a combination of power, beauty, and raw emotion that would make the song stand out and get Pavarotti's attention. "Andrea was just unbelievable," Zucchero said. "He had something not one of the other tenors possessed. He had soul." Bocelli won the audition and made the demo with megastar Zucchero.

Italy's own blues master, Zucchero exploded to stardom in 1987 with his fourth album, *Blues*, which became the best-selling Italian record in history. He followed with *Oro, Incenso & Birra* (*Gold, Incense & Beer*), which was even more successful. He is one of the few Italian pop artists to achieve global fame, and was the only European performer who took part in Woodstock 1994. American audiences also heard him in 1996 and 1997 during sold-out tours to promote his latest albums—tours that brought him to the Los

Zucchero (far right), Italy's answer to the blues and one of its biggest rock stars, invited Bocelli on a European tour to sing the hit duet "Miserere," which Zucchero had recorded with Pavarotti.

Angeles House of Blues and legendary clubs in Chicago and New York. Zucchero was born in 1955 near Reggio Emilia, the historic old city where Bocelli would one day attend the Istituto Cavazza. The first seeds of Zucchero's legendary blend of bold, bluesy rock and ballads were planted when he was introduced to blues music by a visiting American student at his junior high school. He formed his own rhythm-and-blues band at age thirteen, went on the road, and sang his heart out with an unmistakeable raspy and passionate voice that has become a national treasure.

PAVAROTTI LOVED THE SONG AND HE LOVED THE WAY BOCELLI SANG IT. HE TOLD TORPEDINE AND ZUCCHERO, "THIS IS A GREAT TENOR," AND TRIED TO CONVINCE THEM THAT THEY'D BE BETTER OFF USING BOCELLI THAN PAVAROTTI.

Zucchero's agent, Michele Torpedine, flew to Philadelphia to present the demo tape to Pavarotti, who was there working on his international voice competition. Torpedine explained that the guy singing the duet with Zucchero was a piano bar singer from Pisa. The maestro listened to the tape and began to get a little miffed that they were playing games with him. In his mind, the singer was a tenor—not just any tenor, but a very good one. A *great* one, in fact. Why were they trying to convince him that he was just a lounge singer? Pavarotti loved the song and he loved the way Bocelli sang it. He told Torpedine and Zucchero, "This is a great tenor," and tried to convince them that they'd be better off using Bocelli than Pavarotti. In his now-famous remark, which hit the Italian press soon afterward, Pavarotti said, "Thank you for writing such a wonderful song. Yet you do not need me to sing it—let Andrea sing 'Miserere' with you, for there is no one finer."

Torpedine, a former rock-and-roll drummer, didn't have a background in opera or classical music and was surprised that Pavarotti was so impressed with Bocelli. Eventually it sank in that the maestro was quite serious—Bocelli was a voice to be reckoned with. Torpedine had every intention of signing Pavarotti to record the duet and he was confi-

Photo: Allen Malschick/Herbert H. Breslin, Inc.

dent that that would happen, but he was eager to share Pavarotti's words with Bocelli. After the meeting he quickly made a phone call to the unknown piano bar singer to inform him that Luciano Pavarotti thought he was "a great tenor."

Getting the gig in Zucchero's recording studio had seemed fortunate enough, and now Pavarotti had given him his blessing. It sounded too good to be true. To this day, even though he and Pavarotti are now friends, Andrea thinks that the superstar only made that remark to get out of having to do the recording himself. "I have my own opinion of the reason for Maestro Pavarotti's affirmation," said Andrea. "He didn't want to sing it . . . [it] was to get himself out of this." Torpedine insists that Pavarotti was sincere, but Andrea isn't completely sold on the story.

Just as Michele Torpedine predicted, Pavarotti agreed to team up with Zucchero for "Miserere," and the song became an instant hit in Europe. Crowds were screaming to hear the piece when Zucchero hit the concert stage in the summer of 1993, so he asked Bocelli to join him for the European tour. Andrea was soon performing side by side with one of Europe's hottest rock stars. He had also signed with Michele Torpedine, his new manager. The crowd's response to Bocelli during the "Miserere" duet was so overwhelming that Zucchero gave him a solo spot in the show. To everyone's amazement, the rock-and-roll crowd went wild over Andrea's rendition of the aria "Nessun dorma" from Puccini's opera *Turandot*.

The tale of the tape continues. When the European summer tour ended, Zucchero held a birthday party for himself in Modena and invited a who's-who list from Italian pop music, including his new friend Andrea Bocelli. During the festivities that pleasant September evening, the tenor joined in the music-making and sang a few songs at the piano. One of the guests pricked up her ears with interest. She had made a career of discovering new talent and launching these artists through her own record company. That night, Caterina Caselli, founder of Sugar records, knew she had found a new star—a crossover singer who offered something no one had ever heard before. She pulled a contract out of her bag and signed Bocelli on the spot.

Photo © John Barrett/Globe Photos, Inc.

This page, left to right: Michele Torpedine, Andrea Bocelli, Enrica Bocelli, and Alberto Bocelli. Torpedine, Bocelli's manager, was a main force in launching the singer's career and is at the center of Bocelli's current entourage of producers and agents.

Facing page: Luciano Pavarotti played a major role in Bocelli's rise to fame by complimenting his performance on the "Miserere" demo tape. In his now famous remark, which was reported in the Italian press, Pavarotti said that Zucchero didn't need to look any further for a partner for the duet. "Let Andrea sing 'Miserere' with you," he said, "for there is no one finer."

Caterina Caselli has been in the music business since the age of fourteen, when she sang and played bass guitar in a group called Gli Amici (The Friends). The group was very successful and played the major hot spots in Rome and Milan until Caterina made her big break at age twenty singing at the San Remo Festival. The pop star with the distinctive mane of thick, wavy blond hair then launched a movie career, appearing in a string of Italian musicals in the late 1960s. In the next decade she began yet another role in the music industry: that of record producer. The Italian record giant CGD funded her own label, Ascolto (I'm Listening), which focused on young new pop artists. When CGD was sold in 1989, Caterina Caselli Sugar (her new name after marrying Piero Sugar in 1969) took the plunge and started her own record company, Sugar. The very next year the company had a huge hit with "Un'estate italiana" ("An Italian Summer"), the official theme song of the World Football (Soccer) Championship that stayed a number-one Italian hit for nine straight months and topped the charts in Europe and South America as well. Sugar records' first big album successes in the early 1990s were with Paolo Vallesi and Gerardina Trovato, both young stars who made their start when Caterina Caselli Sugar presented them at the San Remo Festival. In addition to running her own record company, Caterina is also the managing editor of Edizioni Suvini Zerboni, a major Italian publisher of both pop and classical music. This position has put her in touch with some of Italy's most eminent classical composers including Goffredo Petrassi and Ennio Morricone, best known in America for his sound tracks for Clint Eastwood westerns such as *A Fistful of Dollars* and *Hang 'em High*.

As soon as Caterina Caselli Sugar signed Bocelli she began to prepare him for the November 1993 preliminary competition of the San Remo Festival. More than any other marketing strategy, record contract, publicity event or talent contest in Italy, the Festival della Canzone Italiana (Italian Song Festival, known simply as the San Remo Festival) is the biggest opportunity for a new pop singer to be seen and heard in Italy.

Presented for the first time in 1951 in a party room in the San Remo Casino, the song festival has become Italian television's biggest event, broadcast live every year from the beautiful resort city on the Italian Riviera. Every year San Remo has presented big stars and introduced new ones who became identified with music from their decade, such as Claudio Villa in the fifties, Catarina Caselli in the sixties, Ricchi o Poveri in the seventies, Eros Ramazzotti and Ana Oxa in the eighties, and Toto Cutugno in the nineties. The television production, viewed by one out of every three Italians, is the most profitable show for Italy's flagship network RAI Uno, and has spawned a series of spin-off shows such as "Aspettando San Remo" ("Awaiting San Remo") and "San Remo Giovani" ("San Remo Youth," the preliminary contest). The popular music festival is truly a "people's choice" award, with winners chosen by large juries made up of viewers from all over Italy. In the main event, which occurs over four days in February, the juries consist of one thousand people between the ages of fourteen and sixty, with the majority of them under thirty. Fifty voters are chosen from each region of the country, and their names are kept secret. There is a new jury for every day of the festival, and on the final two days the size of the juries increases to fifteen hundred, with seventy-five voters chosen from each region. The San

Bocelli with record producer Caterina Caselli Sugar. Caterina signed the singer immediately after hearing him sing at Zucchero's birthday party, and presented him at the prestigious San Remo Festival shortly afterward.

Remo Festival awards winners in two categories: Campioni (Champions), the professional level; and Nuove Proposte (New Talent).

Three months before the main San Remo Festival, referred to as the "Big" competition, Andrea Bocelli performed in the preliminary contest, known as "Giovani." For his entry he sang both parts of the duet "Miserere," something he had done as a joke on the tour with Zucchero. "One evening, after the concert," said Andrea, "we were in an inn for supper and, as happened often, they asked Zucchero to sing something, particularly 'Miserere.' Zucchero was tired and didn't feel like it, and I that evening was well rested and in a very good mood. I walked up to the piano and began to sing it, doing his part as well as mine. This led to such hilarity that, with the unpredictable mind that is my present manager Michele Torpedine, he thought that it would be a good thing to bring it to San Remo. This is how it was born, otherwise I wouldn't have thought of it." Torpedine's hunch was right on target because Bocelli won the preliminary newcomer's contest with the highest marks in the history of the festival.

Part of the joke when Andrea sang "Miserere" for his friends at the inn was his imitation of Zucchero's bluesy voice. When he sang the piece at the festival, he kept some of these stylistic "tricks" in his singing, something he gave up shortly afterward. "[It's] quite dangerous, if one repeats it often, to use the voice like the 'blues men,' " he said. "It can be dangerous for the voice, for the vocal cords." After the success with "Miserere," Andrea recalled, "my record company and my team in general thought that it would be interesting to repeat this experiment. I said that a game should not last too long, that one had succeeded and that was the end of that." Bocelli wouldn't allow himself to be molded into a singer with a pocketful of artificial techniques that served the pop style, not the voice.

The "Miserere" victory allowed Bocelli to move up to the "Big" show in February, where he sang the love ballad "Il mare calmo della sera" ("The Calm Evening Sea"), accompanied by a full orchestra. Caterina Caselli Sugar had discovered the song and she invited Andrea to try it out in her office one day. He showed up with his father and sang it through, and the record producer knew that Andrea had the melting romantic quality that would make the song a success. She was right. On the night of his festival appearance in February 1995, with millions of Italians watching, Andrea Bocelli sang "Il mare calmo della sera" and became a famous man. His performance brought the audience to their feet and he took first place in the New Talent category. As with his history-making performance at the preliminary concert, Andrea also broke the scoring record at the main festival with the highest marks ever awarded by the nationwide jury in this category. The people had spoken—Andrea Bocelli was a star.

Going to San Remo had been a big dream during Bocelli's years in the piano bars. For years his family and friends had urged him to go, but not until he met Zucchero and Caterina Caselli Sugar did he feel compelled to try. Winning the festival competition proved that his decision to quit his law career was okay, that he had made the right choice in devoting himself to music. "In that moment," Andrea said of his winning night, "I thought of all of my friends who always believed in me, of all those who always said I should go to San Remo, and most of all of my parents, who were there at that moment. I believe . . . that evening . . . they understood my 'mania,' this desire to win this bet in life and to make a life from music."

Andrea's demo tape had brought him to the inner circle of Italian pop music, and it would soon bring him to an even wider television audience. After his win in San Remo, Andrea received the late-night call from Luciano Pavarotti. When his head finally cleared and the shock wore off, he understood that the maestro wanted Andrea to join him and a lineup of stars for his next "Pavarotti and Friends" concert. The show would be televised live throughout Europe from a magnificent outdoor amphitheater in Pavarotti's hometown, Modena.

Pavarotti and Zucchero came up with the idea of a classical/pop benefit concert to raise funds for various children's charities in 1992. Since then they've raised millions of dollars by producing concerts in which Pavarotti sings duets and shares the stage with pop and rock stars such as Sting, Liza Minnelli, Bryan Adams, Bono, Michael Bolton, Brian Eno, Stevie Wonder, the Spice Girls, and Celine Dion. Never before had the classical and pop/rock worlds been brought together on such a scale and so successfully. "Pavarotti and Friends" has become an annual event and one of the most popular live television shows in Europe.

Bocelli's solo piece for the September 1994 concert was "Mattinata," a song by Ruggero Leoncavallo, composer of the popular opera *I Pagliacci*. Leoncavallo is best known for that opera, but "Mattinata" was a frequent selection in Enrico Caruso's concerts. Caruso also recorded the song early in his career, with the composer accompanying

ANDREA SPENT A WEEK WITH PAVAROTTI BEFORE THE CONCERT AND THE TWO FORMED A CLOSE, WARM FRIENDSHIP BASED ON A MUTUAL LOVE OF MUSIC AND HORSES. IN PAVAROTTI ANDREA BOCELLI FOUND A NEW SOURCE OF SUPPORT AND ENCOURAGEMENT.

him at the piano. Bocelli's other appearances on the program were a duet with Pavarotti, "Notte e piscatore" by M. Morante; a sextet with Pavarotti, Bryan Adams, Andreas Vollenweider, Italian pop singer Giorgia, and soprano Nancy Gustafson on Bryan Adams's song "All for Love"; and with the same sextet singing the "Brindisi" from Verdi's *La Traviata*.

Andrea spent a week with Pavarotti before the concert and the two formed a close, warm friendship based on a mutual love of music and horses. In Pavarotti Andrea Bocelli found a new source of support and encouragement that bolstered his enthusiasm about working on his voice. "It is very important to know that someone like Pavarotti believes in you," he said.

Bocelli's win at San Remo automatically placed him in the professional "Big" competition the following year. He entered with a new song by Francesco Sartori and Lucio Quarantotto, "Con te partirò" ("I Will Go with You," translated as "Time to Say Goodbye"). It was a great song that would eventually make him practically a household name throughout the world, but on that February evening in 1995 he was more nervous than usual. "I was distracted due to an important event," he said. "I was about to become a father." Enrica was in the hospital in Pontedera, two hundred miles away, delivering their first child. Andrea was crazed with anxiety and anticipation over what was happening at the hospital and couldn't focus on his performance. "I remember that my mother came in the dressing room and said to me, 'Everything is fine' . . . [but] obviously, you can't concentrate much under circumstances like these." Bocelli took fourth place in the festival, behind first-place champion Giorgia, who won with the song "Saprei," second-place duo Gianni Morandi and Barbara Cola, and third-place winner Spagna.

Even though "Con te partirò" didn't become a hit after San Remo, Andrea had complete faith in the song. He knew its day would come. "I even told my record company," Andrea said in 1999, "[that] 'Con te partirò' was a marathon runner. It could not run at San Remo, which is a hundred-meter sprint. Still, five years after the song came out it is still very much loved and still continues to sell. There is nothing phony about it, nothing tricky. There are not too many songs in the world like this. Only five or six songs like this are born in a century."

Bocelli's San Remo appearances led to his first albums for the Sugar label: *Il Mare Calmo della Sera* in 1994 and *Bocelli* in 1995. Just as Andrea had predicted, "Con te partirò" found the right race to run as a single from the *Bocelli* album. It tore up the charts all over Europe, including Belgium, where it became the biggest hit in history, spending twelve weeks in the number-one spot; in France, where it stayed on the top of the charts for six weeks; and in Germany, where it sold nearly two million copies in a matter of weeks. But just like a great distance runner, "Con te partirò" was just warming up.

Sarah Brightman heard the song in a restaurant one evening while dining out with friends. Smitten, she tracked down the CD and called Bocelli personally to ask him if he would perform the song with her in a duet version for an upcoming appearance in Germany. Brightman, a veteran of the London musical stage since childhood, achieved international fame performing in works such as *Cats, The Phantom of the Opera,* and the concert piece *Requiem* by Andrew Lloyd Webber, to whom she was married for several years. Like Bocelli, Sarah Brightman has successfully combined classical and pop music in a career that includes classical albums such as the *Requiem,* which earned her a Grammy nomination as Best New Classical Artist, and *Eden,* her recent album of eclectic songs featuring serene, electronically enhanced arrangements.

The performance that Brightman wished to do with Andrea involved one of her close friends, German boxing champion Henry Maske. The previous year, after completing a concert tour of Germany, she had sung at the introduction to Maske's world championship title match, which was televised in many countries. Henry Maske, a 1988 Olympic Gold Medalist and national hero nicknamed the "Gentleman," is renowned for entering the ring to a well-chosen piece of music that will thrill the crowd. Sarah Brightman's performance of "Question of Honor" had been such a hit in 1995 that Maske invited her to return in 1996 for his farewell match against United States light-heavyweight champion Virgil Hill. Andrea agreed to do the performance and looked forward to meeting the athlete about whom he had heard so much. He instantly felt a rapport with Maske: "When we first shook hands," said Bocelli, "we knew that there was something connecting

Bocelli gets a bear hug from German boxing champion Henry Maske. The boxer's internationally televised farewell match featured a live performance of Bocelli and Sarah Brightman singing "Time to Say Goodbye," the new duet version of Bocelli's huge hit "Con te partirò."

Photo © Agenzia ANSA

us. . . . [It was] very spontaneous, a wonderful friendship between two entirely different human beings developed."

At the match, Maske lost to Virgil Hill on a point decision after twelve rounds, but the crowd didn't need a win to pay an emotional tribute to their beloved star of the ring. Bocelli and Brightman sang the fitting "Time to Say Goodbye" during the closing ceremony as Maske said farewell to his fans in the arena and in the television audience. The astounding response to the song by the boxing fans was matched only by the success of the recording, a single that had recently been made by Bocelli and Brightman and was released soon after the fight. The duet, recorded with the London Symphony Orchestra, shot to the number-one spot in Germany and stayed there for fourteen weeks, selling one million more copies than Bocelli's solo version. "Time to Say Goodbye" became the best-selling single of all time in Germany as well as Switzerland, and it quickly climbed the charts in France and the rest of Europe as well. "Who could have seen that right after this such a huge fervor for this song would be unleashed?" mused Bocelli. "There's always some hidden reason for things that happen."

By the autumn of 1997, Andrea Bocelli was the new voice of light popular music in Europe with two hit singles and three albums, *Il Mare Calmo della Sera* from 1994 and *Bocelli* and *Viaggio Italiano* from 1995. To round out the success of that year, Michele Torpedine sent Bocelli on a tour with the annual Night of the Proms tour in Europe. A concert event very popular with all ages, Night of the Proms takes its name from London's legendary Proms concerts, which have been bringing classical music to large crowds in a strictly un-concert-hall atmosphere every July for over one hundred years. In London, at the concert appropriately called The Last Night of the Proms, a Mahler symphony or other timeless warhorse turns Royal Albert Hall into nothing less than a love-fest of humanity. Like their English cousin, the continental Night of the Proms concerts feature a full symphony orchestra and a large chorus, but with the addition of a full rock band up front. Unlike the London Proms, these concerts are a blend of classical and pop usually headlined by international pop stars rather than opera divas or concert pianists. In the summer of 1995 Andrea shared the Night of the Proms stage with stars such as American blues singer John Miles, Bryan Ferry, and Al Jarreau, who later remarked that Bocelli had "the most beautiful voice in the world." The tour played in Holland, Belgium, Germany, Spain, and France, each night accompanied by the Novecento Orchestra of Belgium. Andrea provided the classical side of that season's Night of the Proms, performing a variety of arias. These appearances brought Bocelli before nearly five hundred thousand people, provided great publicity for his new recordings, and earned him even more fans.

For better or worse, touring would become a regular part of Andrea Bocelli's life. It takes him away from home, sometimes away from his family, and also takes enormous energy. A three-month summer tour of outdoor concerts in Germany in 1997, for example, drew huge crowds but terrible weather, with hundreds of people sitting in soaked dress clothes and stomping through the mud to leave before the lightning storms began. Performing and traveling in a long stretch of wet weather drains everyone's energy. Some of Bocelli's happiest moments in concert and on the road, however, would have been

Andrea Bocelli meeting Pope John Paul II after a performance in Bologna. Singing in the presence of Il Papa has been a very emotional experience for Bocelli, and something he considers one the greatest benefits of his fame. "In circumstances like these," he said, "your life passes by you."

bright regardless the weather.

In August 1997, Bocelli was invited to perform at the annual Puccini Festival, one of the opera world's favorite summer festivals, held at the Puccini villa in Torre del Lago. This lakeside festival, about five miles (eight kilometers) north of Pisa, attracts millions of people every summer between late July and mid-August. The festival was founded in 1930, six years after Puccini's death, and offers three operas each season as well as concerts and lectures. Music lovers are also drawn to the festival to visit the museumlike villa itself, inhabited now by Puccini's granddaughter, Simonetta Puccini. Andrea Bocelli performed in Torre del Lago's famous Teatro di Quattromila (Theater of Four Thousand), an immense stage platform built on the edge of the lake. During performances, four thousand spectators face the serene lake where Puccini spent many happy hours fishing and shooting ducks. Andrea had attended the festival when he was a boy, and it was here that he first heard Franco Corelli in a live opera, *La Bohème*. The opera star would one day become Bocelli's teacher and mentor. Singing Puccini arias at Torre del Lago during those summer evenings in 1997 was a rich experience for Bocelli, who has always felt a deep-rooted connection with Puccini and the countryside he loved. Perhaps the most moving and personally meaningful concert appearances Andrea has made, however, are those in which he

PERHAPS THE MOST MOVING AND PERSONALLY MEANINGFUL CONCERT APPEARANCES ANDREA HAS MADE ARE THOSE IN WHICH HE SANG BEFORE THE POPE.

sang before the Pope. Between 1994 and 1997 Andrea had three opportunities to sing for Il Papa. During Christmas of 1994 he sang "Adeste Fideles" in St. Peter's Basilica in Vatican City; in August 1997 he participated in the World Youth Festival in Paris before the Pope; and in September of that year he sang for a Catholic congress attended by the Pope in Bologna. Bocelli performed in the Vatican again in the autumn of 1997 for "Telefood," a spectacular televised benefit concert that raised funds to feed needy children and families. For the Bologna concert, the tenor sang "Nessun dorma" from *Turandot*. One of the most compelling arias in all of opera, ending with a glorious high B on the word vincerò ("I will win"), "Nessun dorma" is Pavarotti's signature aria and a no-fail "goose-bump" piece. Andrea had already sung it to much acclaim in concerts with Zucchero, and he felt that it would help express the goal of the Catholic gathering. "We wanted to find a piece that was popular," Bocelli said, "but at the same time represented victory, hope . . . [a song] that would give a message, and 'Nessun dorma' represented all of this."

On July 30, 1999, Bocelli was once again invited to sing for the Pope, this time for an audition rather than a performance. He traveled to Castel Gandolfo, the Pope's summer palace outside Rome, to sing "Hymn of the 2000 Holy Year," which is to be performed during the Jubilee ceremony at the Vatican in December 1999. Thereafter, the hymn will be sung in Catholic parishes throughout the world as the theme song of the Church's third millennium. If Bocelli is chosen to sing the hymn, it will undoubtedly put him in front of the largest live and television audience of his career.

Andrea admitted to being very nervous before each of these performances for the

Holy Father. "It was difficult, but [of] great satisfaction . . . [and] strong emotion, because I am Catholic. In circumstances like these," he said, "your life passes by you." Recalling the moment he met the Pope for the first time, Andrea said, "I do not know how to express the emotion I felt. He encouraged me very warmly." Bocelli reflected on this meeting and the benefit concerts as life experiences worth waiting for. "To achieve success," he said, "it is necessary to have a large component of luck. I have enough; however, at the beginning things were very bad for me. And in this sense, the road has been very difficult. But in the end, when destiny placed me in front of the Pope, great things resulted."

The traveling that is demanded for his tours, which began in 1993 with Zucchero and continue with the release of each new album, is the biggest price Bocelli has to pay for his career. Sitting for hours in an airplane is almost unbearable for the athletic tenor, whose favorite mode of transportation is a horse and who suffers from recurring back problems. Whenever possible he returns to the seashore or the country, gets back on a horse, and lives the good life for a few precious days. Bocelli has always been a very active, sports-loving person who needs to connect with the outdoors. Whether it's an evening stroll, swimming, skiing, bicycle riding, or keeping up with the latest games of his favorite soccer teams, he's enthusiastic about sports and keeps as active as possible. He learned to ski from a master, his friend and Olympic gold medalist Alberto Tomba. They ski side by side down Italy's slopes, Andrea holding one end of a ski pole and Alberto holding the other.

Andrea Bocelli has his own gauge of riskiness when it comes to sports, but his family doesn't always share his confidence. He and his father were out for a drive one afternoon,

Bocelli with his friend, Italian skier and Olympic gold medalist Alberto Tomba. They ski side by side down the slopes, each holding one end of a ski pole.

Photo © SYGMA

and they came upon a small airport where a local parachuting group was getting ready to take off. "They asked me if I wanted to do it," said Andrea, "And I said, 'I have the whole afternoon, sure, let's try it.' " His father wasn't as excited about the idea, however. "My *babbo* was with me," Andrea said. "Obviously, we were not really very much in agreement that I should do this thing." If Enrica had been along, things wouldn't have gone far at all. "She has said that if she had been there she would not have let me jump," Andrea said. But in her absence, Andrea and the rest of the team assured Sandro Bocelli that his son would be safe. He suited up, strapped on a parachute and a helmet, and hopped into the plane.

The jump was a complete success and he's never regretted it. "It is a sensation one cannot describe; one must try it," he said.

Andrea discovered the joys of skiing later in life, but he learned how to ride the hilly roads of Tuscany on a bicycle in his childhood. He still rides along busy Italian roads today, putting his complete trust in Italian drivers to keep a close watch and give him room. Andrea appreciates sports and the exercise he gets from swimming and bicycle riding for practical reasons, too. "Sport is an irreplaceable part of my life," he said. "When you want to be at the highest level as a singer, you have to make sure you are in perfect condition."

"SPORT IS AN IRREPLACEABLE PART OF MY LIFE," ANDREA SAID. "WHEN YOU WANT TO BE AT THE HIGHEST LEVEL AS A SINGER, YOU HAVE TO MAKE SURE YOU ARE IN PERFECT CONDITION."

Bocelli hasn't changed his hobbies, his friends, his priorities, or his attitude throughout his rise to fame. These qualities were well in place by the time the wheel of fortune began to turn in his direction, and he's grateful to have an inner foundation that keeps his personal life intact. "Luckily, my biggest fortune is that I found a serenity and a peace before I began this career," he said. "I'm very happy with life. I would never say to myself that 'I've arrived,' or 'I'm there.' I've never measured my success and I don't think I ever will."

Andrea Bocelli made his opera debut at the Teatro Verdi in Pisa, home of the Pisa Opera Theater. Built in 1865, this nine-hundred-seat theater is the cultural center of the city. One of the main goals of the opera company is to give young singers the opportunity to perform their first roles in a nurturing, supportive, yet highly professional atmosphere.

Photos: Susan Turner

Opera
or
Pop?
4

LIRICA O LEGGERA? asked dozens of Italian headlines after Bocelli's first appearance on the opera stage. Is the star of the San Remo pop music festival a lyric (opera/stage) singer or a crooner of light, popular music? The fact that Bocelli was becoming wildly popular in Europe and America stumped many in the Italian music industry because his fame in Italy didn't begin to measure up to such pop superstars as Zucchero and Eros Ramazotti. How could a newcomer like Bocelli find global success as an Italian artist before establishing himself as a star at home? This backwards type of success had no precedent. "It would be funny," wrote *Il Tirreno*, the newspaper from Pontedera (near Bocelli's home), "if, unlike Zucchero, Laura Pausini, and Eros Ramazzotti, Andrea Bocelli first conquered the rest of the world and then his fellow countrymen." Every pop singer's dream is to be heard and loved beyond his or her national borders, and the road to such international recognition is usually a long one. Oddly, Bocelli was already there.

Further complicating the issue was Bocelli's appearance in both the pop and opera worlds. To most musicians, opera and pop are two different universes, yet Bocelli dove headfirst into both in 1994. Just weeks after making his mark at the San Remo Festival, one of the high points of any Italian pop singer's career, he stunned everyone by showing up in a production of Verdi's *Macbeth* at the Teatro Verdi in Pisa. It was an official step into the hallowed halls of opera, which in Italy, perhaps more than anywhere else, is serious cultural business. In response to the question of "lirica o leggera," Andrea had two major points to make: his popular music was a vehicle for bringing people to his real music, opera; and singing popular music was a natural course that had been taken by other Italian tenors of the past.

Even though Andrea isn't primarily interested in popular music, he respects it for the role it plays in bringing people to his concerts. Pop, in his opinion, may not measure up to opera, but it serves a very important purpose in his ultimate musical goal. *Romanza* and *Sogno* bring sellout crowds to his live performances, in which he sings only classical music. "What I want to do is to take people by the hand and gently lead them to opera," Bocelli said. "Pop music is my legs, classical music my heart. But I need my legs to get to where I want to go."

Andrea Bocelli is adamant about spreading his love for opera. Bringing this art form to a large audience is his prime objective, his biggest motivator, his life mission. "If just three young people in the audience are converted to classical, then it's a success," he said about his live concerts. "I will continue to do it if it brings classical music nearer to the younger generations." With the unexpected success of his popular albums, Bocelli feels he is in a unique position to serve his art—classical music—which he considers native to his country. "Music is an Italian thing," he said. "Music was born in Italy." His enthusiasm for the musical heritage of Italy overflows into his performances and motivates his career. The popular songs in his recordings are sung in the original Italian because Bocelli wants to "capture the American market, but in my language." He says: "It's true that I sang one song in English and that was arduous for me. But the rest is in Italian because to me it seems important to be able to export the culture of a small country with such a big musical tradition."

The Bocelli mission of bringing opera to the masses applies to his own country, too, where he hopes to bring a new generation to an old art form. Referring to his performances in *La Bohème* in Cagliari as well as to an opera concert that followed, Bocelli said, "In Cagliari there were many young people and children. I have been told that the same thing occurred last Sunday in the National Auditorium [in Rome]. I don't know if they will become opera fans, but at least they now know that opera exists."

With feet planted firmly in both pop and opera, Bocelli sees no reason for giving up one for the other. "Operatic music is the music that I love. I have the desire to sing that which I like myself, but I will always make such albums as *Romanza* because they are important for bringing my public closer to my true music." Inspired and honestly surprised by the excellent sales of *Aria*, which contains no popular music, Bocelli is convinced that his mission is on track. "The fact that [*Aria*] is classical, with opera arias, and making these [sales] numbers is surprising to us. This is important, however, because it means that slowly, slowly, people come to opera. Probably many of them will come to the theater; they will learn to really appreciate the opera, and this is the thing that makes me happy more than anything."

Bocelli's second point about the virtue of recording pop albums rests upon the tradition of some of Italy's most famous tenors. Everyone who asks Andrea about the gulf between opera and pop is given a short lesson in opera singing: "All the tenors throughout history turned to the popular repertory to approach the public, without losing their passion for the classic," he said. "I am in that line." The public's love for a beautiful, classically trained voice was carefully groomed in the twentieth century by a handful of artists who presented a mix of popular and classical music. Bocelli, who has listened to recordings of famous tenors since childhood, is completely at home in this tradition. "I am very much influenced by other singers before me who were able to interpret popular repertoires as well as the most difficult works. I am reminded of Caruso, who when he sang Neapolitan songs would generate the same phenomenon as the Three Tenors today. Or when Beniamino Gigli appeared in films where he sang great hits such as 'Mamma, son tanto felice.' "

A handful of today's opera stars have reached out into nonoperatic music after establishing themselves in opera. Soprano Kiri Te Kanawa, mezzo-soprano Marilyn Horn, and tenor José Carreras, for example, made a famous recording of Leonard Bernstein's *West*

PLÁCIDO DOMINGO HAS RECORDED POPULAR SONGS IN BOTH SPANISH AND ENGLISH, INCLUDING A VERY SUCCESSFUL ALBUM WITH JOHN DENVER CALLED PERHAPS LOVE. LIKE BOCELLI, HE IS GRATIFIED THAT THESE POPULAR ALBUMS HELP BRING A NEW AUDIENCE TO OPERA.

Side Story, conducted by the composer. Plácido Domingo has recorded popular songs in both Spanish and English, including a very successful album with John Denver called *Perhaps Love*. Like Bocelli, he is gratified that these popular albums help bring a new audience to opera. With popular albums, says Domingo, "I can sing for and be appreciated by people who do not enjoy opera; and . . . I am helping to stimulate interest in opera." After the release of *Perhaps Love,* Domingo received many letters from fans saying that the album had motivated them to go to the opera for the first time, and they loved it. Even though Andrea Bocelli is traveling in the opposite direction—famous for his popular albums before making a name for himself in opera—both tenors share a common goal.

Tenors such as Caruso, his successor Gigli, and America's own Mario Lanza helped cultivate the public's ear for bel canto, beautiful singing. The luminary tenors of this century ignited a frenzy among audiences with powerful voices that made the listener's body ring with resonance and emotion. When sung by a Caruso or Corelli, a popular ballad could deliver the same emotional punch as a classic melody from Puccini or Verdi. There is an intensity and passion to the lyric and dramatic Italian tenor voice that can stir an audience unlike anything else. Enrico Caruso, Beniamino Gigli, Mario Del Monaco, Giuseppe di Stefano, Franco Corelli, and Luciano Pavarotti are some of the tenors who, like forces of nature, have shaken theaters with thrilling high Cs and unforgettable voices. The great Italian tenors hold an exalted place in Italy and in the history of opera.

As a child, Andrea Bocelli was drawn to opera recordings with a deep and natural affection for singing that his parents couldn't explain. By the time he was old enough to study music in school, the sound of legendary voices like those of Caruso and Corelli were imprinted in his brain and on his soul. Over Bocelli's lifetime, a handful of singers have become an ideal, a testament to great singing and the beauty it can bring to the world.

First on this list of singers is Enrico Caruso (1873–1921), the tenor who single-handedly ushered in the golden age of Italian tenors. Caruso's expressiveness, depth of feeling, and aggressive approach to singing keep him in a class by himself with many opera aficionados to this day, including Andrea Bocelli. Caruso's voice was perfectly suited to the new type of opera being created by the composers of his time such as Puccini, Pietro Mascagni, and Ruggiero Leoncavallo. These composers were building upon the realism and drama that Verdi had recently ignited in opera—changing the art form forever. Caruso's ability to create hair-raising theater with his voice was tailor-made for this new dramatic style. Not only did he perform the roles that defined verismo (realism—opera that portrays violent passions and actions), he helped develop this operatic style by giving composers new ideas about what the tenor voice could do. Legend has it that Caruso, shortly after performing in Puccini's *La Bohème* for the first time, visited the composer at his home near Lucca. Puccini sat down at the piano and invited the tenor to sing through one of the arias from the opera. Caruso had sung only a few phrases when Puccini jumped up and exclaimed: "Who sent you to me—God?"

In addition to hard-hitting, melodramatic operas that showcased his dramatic flair and large voice, Caruso had the benefit of a new invention, the phonograph, to make him one of the biggest celebrities of his time. His first recording was made in Milan in 1902 by the Gramophone and Typewriter Company of London, and he went on to make more than 230 record-

Some of Andrea's earliest memories are of listening to recordings of Enrico Caruso, the Italian tenor who helped usher in a new era in Italian opera. Caruso's aggressive, dramatic style and powerful high notes made a deep and lasting impression on Bocelli as well as on countless other singers and opera lovers.

Photo: Archives of Antonia Felix

ings before his death at age forty-eight in 1921. He spent eighteen seasons at the Metropolitan Opera in New York, the city that he made a home base with a fourteen-room suite at the Hotel Knickerbocker.

Caruso's concert programs almost always included a popular song or two. In a special concert given at the Metropolitan Opera to benefit the families of the victims of the *Titanic* in 1912, he sang Sir Arthur Sullivan's heart-tugging "The Lost Chord." During World War I he happily turned to American popular music in benefit concerts, where huge crowds would flock to hear him sing the zippy "Over There," written by his friend George M. Cohan. He was also often requested to perform "The Star Spangled Banner" during the war years. Caruso was renowned for his generosity and larger-than-life personality, which fueled the characterizations he produced on stage. After Caruso's death it was discovered that, in addition to spending a fortune on Christmas gifts for everyone in the theater each year and supporting many relatives back in Italy, he had been providing regular financial support to more than 120 people for many years.

Caruso created a new level of excitement in opera, and new expectations. One of his true heirs was Beniamino Gigli (1890–1957), an Italian tenor who, in his first seasons at the Met, lived in Caruso's shadow. Andrea Bocelli has described Gigli as "the most famous tenor in the world," and throughout his life he has listened to recordings of the great singer from Recanati. Gigli's voice was smooth, sweet, strong, and vital. He took listeners' breath away with floating *pianissimi* (extremely quiet/soft notes) and he sprinkled sentimental phrases with heart-wrenching sobs. Enjoying a long career at the

Metropolitan Opera—one that overlapped briefly with Caruso's—he inherited Caruso's less dramatic roles. Like Caruso, Gigli was very comfortable performing popular music, and his recordings of songs such as "Mamma" and "Se vuoi goder la vita" became big hits. Gigli was proud to consider himself "the people's singer," always eager to include many love songs and popular standards in his concerts and recordings. His fame spread to an even wider audience when he became a singing cinema idol in such movies as *Ave Maria*, *Solo per te* (*Only for You*), and *Mamma* (for which the previously mentioned hit songs were written) in the 1930s. Thanks to his popular music and many films, Gigli was a celebrity tenor who enjoyed fame equal to Pavarotti's today.

The Neapolitan songs sung and recorded by Caruso, Gigli and Lanza still work their magic with modern audiences. The Three Tenors have roused stadium-size crowds with "O sole mio," a song recognized by everyone—including children—throughout the world, and one of the songs Andrea recorded on *Viaggio Italiano*. The pleasant melodies and romantic lyrics of Neapolitan songs, tunes from the nineteenth century by composers such as Eduardo di Capua, Francesco Tosti, and Ernesto De Curtis, have given them staying power that rivals favorite opera arias.

Andrea compares the popular music of his recordings, from Neapolitan songs to new pieces written by his friend Lucio Quarantotto, to the hits that made Caruso and Gigli two of the most important figures in bringing opera to a wider public. He understands the irresistible draw of a beautiful melody and touching words. When it comes to the power of popular song, "there is nothing like 'O sole mio' or 'Con te partirò,' " Bocelli said. "It was

Photo: Marcello Garofalo

Another legendary tenor idolized by Bocelli is Beniamino Gigli, one of the most famous singers in operatic history and a true heir to Caruso. Andrea often refers to Gigli as the perfect example of an opera star who switched easily from opera to popular love songs and ballads, and who popularized opera through performing lighter styles of music as well as appearing in films.

like Gigli who gained popularity with 'Mamma,' or like Caruso for whom 'Core ingrato' was written by two Italian-Americans. It is typical of our tenors." Love songs, especially when transformed with lush orchestrations, pull out all the romantic stops, regardless of the decade in which they were written. Bocelli understands this. If romantic pop music has one thing in common with certain operas such as *La Bohème* or *Cavalleria Rusticana,* it is a focus on romance, relationships, and sensuality. Bocelli, like any good recording star, understands that romance is irresistible: "I believe that one of the most fundamental aspects of people, and of course of singers, is sensuality." Popular songs have the power to tap into this quality, Bocelli believes, because pop is "based more on the art of communication and fantasy."

Another tenor who communicated through both pop and opera, and whose fame with American audiences demands a comparison to Bocelli, is the legendary Mario Lanza

(1921–1959). Before the superstardom of Pavarotti—on his own and as one of the Three Tenors—America went through a phase of tenor-worship at the feet of the Italian-style tenor, son of Italian immigrant parents. This handsome, charming hunk from the tough streets of Philadelphia did more to bring opera to the American public through his movies, television appearances, and recordings than any other singer before or since. As Bocelli's record sales and concert appearances eclipse the Three Tenors, he is being compared to Mario Lanza as a great popularizer of opera, especially in the United States.

AS BOCELLI'S RECORD SALES AND CONCERT APPEARANCES ECLIPSE THE THREE TENORS, HE IS BEING COMPARED TO MARIO LANZA AS A GREAT POPULARIZER OF OPERA, ESPECIALLY IN THE UNITED STATES.

Like Bocelli, Mario Lanza had an early love for opera that wasn't shared by his friends. By age ten his favorite piece of music was the aria "Vesti la giubba" from *I Pagliacci*, one of the selections on a Caruso album that he listened to constantly. He had already decided that he wanted to sing like Caruso, but it was a dream that he kept to himself throughout his school years. When he wasn't playing football or boxing or working out at the South Philadelphia Boys Weight-Lifting Club, he was at home listening to recordings of Caruso. His parents scrimped and saved to buy him standing-room opera tickets, and he always went alone. He didn't begin to take voice lessons until he was twenty years old, and he got his first opera training at the summer festival in Tanglewood in

Photo: Archives of Antonia Felix

Mario Lanza captured the hearts of America singing opera and popular music in his renowned concerts at the Hollywood Bowl and other large venues as well as in movies such as The Student Prince *and* The Great Caruso. *The darkly handsome Hollywood idol created a new generation of opera fans and inspired classical artists such as José Carreras, Plácido Domingo, and Luciano Pavarotti. Bocelli's enormous popularity and ability to introduce operatic music to the general public in the United States recall Lanza's career and legacy.*

1942 (another musician at the festival that year, also destined to become a legend in American music, was a young conductor named Leonard Bernstein). Good reviews for Lanza's performance in *The Merry Wives of Windsor* almost got his career rolling, but the draft intervened. Not long after being described by the *New York Times* as a young talent "whose superb natural voice has few equals among tenors of the day in quality, warmth and power," Lanza suddenly found himself in Texas as an M.P. in the Army. Fortunately, the singer came to the attention of the right people and was given time off to perform in national shows such as "On the Beam" and "Winged Victory." These appearances made him a darling of his movie-star colleagues and Hollywood, which would successfully lure him away from the concert career he built after the War.

Films such as *Serenade, The Student Prince, Because You're Mine, The Great Caruso,* and *The Toast of New Orleans* spawned many hit songs and created a massive following for Lanza's classical and popular albums. Fans bought Mario Lanza records for his popular songs including "Be My Love," "They Didn't Believe Me," "Arrivederci Roma," and "Because You're Mine," as well as for opera arias such as "Vesti la giubba," "Una furtiva lagrima," and "La donna è mobile." His voice was renowned for its size as well as its warmth, and it has been admired by famous opera singers including José Carreras, Plácido Domingo, and Luciano Pavarotti. Another respected figure in the classical music world, conductor Arturo Toscanini, declared in the 1940s that Lanza possessed perhaps the greatest natural voice of the century. Forty years after his death, Mario Lanza continues to inspire singers and opera lovers—and draw crowds. Young American tenor Richard Leech, one of today's big international opera stars, has performed tribute concerts in Chicago and Cincinnati, reproducing Lanza's own concert programs. "It was Mario Lanza, booming from my parents' hi-fi, that was my first exposure not only to opera but to the tenor voice itself," he said. The outstanding response to these concerts, as well as the continuing demand for Lanza records, shows that public interest in Lanza has not faded.

Andrea Bocelli's sold-out stadium concerts draw the same response as Lanza's performances. Lanza was idolized by all ages, and the response from Bocelli's concerts is reminiscent of those crowds. Steven Mercurio, who conducted Bocelli's first thirteen American concerts as well as his *La Bohème* and other performances, was amazed at the audience frenzy during Bocelli's first American tour in 1998. "The response was crazy. The crowd's screaming and applause when Andrea came out, after he finished a song, and for encores had a rock-and-roll environment to it. It was a very strange mix of people from very young to very old. The Three Tenors elicit this sort of response, but this was even more. There were a lot of people from the ages of say forty to sixty-five who weren't 'opera people.' The Three Tenors drew mostly opera people. Every night I would go out there and laugh at what was going on. I was always trying to explain the scene to Andrea, leaning over and talking to him between songs."

They were clapping, whistling, and yelling for arias. Bocelli included one pop song, "Con te partirò," in his concerts, but the rest of the program was strictly classical. *Romanza* had brought them to the show, but Andrea's opera arias brought them to their feet.

Bocelli's desire to build a career as an opera singer, performing in full productions in opera houses, contrasts Mario Lanza's goals. At his death at age thirty-eight in 1959, Lanza had sung in only two staged operas, the Tanglewood performance and a *Madama Butterfly* with the New Orleans Opera. Lanza didn't have the discipline for performing in the theater, nor the desire. He concentrated on his fabulous Hollywood Bowl concerts, his movies, and his recordings. Traipsing the boards of the opera stage was low on his list of priorities. Not so with Andrea Bocelli.

In the summer of 1994, Andrea had made his first move toward the opera stage—an audition for a role at the Teatro Verdi in nearby Pisa. The perfect opportunity awaited him in the opera company at this theater, which devoted itself entirely to giving young singers a chance to perform their first roles. Andrea knew that the company had scheduled a production of Verdi's *Macbeth*, an opera that contains the part of Macduff, the perfect role for a novice yet earnest young tenor. Although Macduff is not one of the leading roles, the character plays a vital part in the drama and has one beautiful aria in the fourth act. Andrea contacted the artistic director of the theater, Claudio Desderi, and asked to be allowed to audition for the part. Before meeting Andrea, Desderi was impressed by the singer's seriousness and his enthusiasm about performing his first role. Always ready to support a talented young musician, Desderi agreed to schedule an audition.

Pisa's Teatro Verdi was developing a special training program for aspiring opera singers, which has now become the Course for the Professional Development of Singers (Corso di Formazione Professionale per Cantanti). Although the program wasn't in full swing when Andrea auditioned for *Macbeth*, some aspects were already under way, such as outreach workshops in the local schools and community to heighten interest in the opera. *Macbeth* and other productions at Teatro Verdi have attracted many teenagers who, fresh from classes about the background of the opera, are anxious to see the real thing. The young artist training course now receives about one hundred applications each year, but only twenty-five applicants are accepted. This keeps the classes small and guarantees that each student will have an opportunity to perform in a fully staged opera in the jewel-like, 135-year-old theater. Similar young artist programs are offered by opera companies in the United States, such as the San Francisco Opera Center's Merola Opera Program, Lyric Opera of Chicago's Lyric Opera Center for American Artists, Houston Grand Opera's Houston Opera Studio, and the Metropolitan Opera's Young Artist Development

Program. These highly competitive apprenticeship programs are an important part of the singing actor's professional training—along with study at a university or conservatory.

When conductor Claudio Desderi met Andrea for the first time at the audition in Pisa, he was impressed. As a veteran of the opera stage, Desderi knows voices. He recognizes talent, dedication, and a singer's capacity for discipline and hard work—absolute requirements for an opera career.

"Andrea made an audition for me before he became a star," said Desderi. "His voice was very nice, very cultivated. I found him very interesting and talented as a young tenor, and I offered him the part of Macduff in the production of *Macbeth*."

Desderi is a conductor and artistic director who understands the unique demands and challenges of singing on stage. His wisdom comes from experience: before launching his conducting career in 1991, Desderi spent twenty-two years singing bass roles in the world's major opera houses. In addition to performing many years at the Lyric Opera of Chicago, he was a well-known artist in such opera houses as London's Covent Garden, the Paris Opéra, and the Metropolitan Opera in New York, where he sang the role of Bartolo in Rossini's *The Barber of Seville* in the 1988–1989 season. Desderi brought a wealth of experience and a world-class standard of singing to his young artists at the Pisa theater, as he has worked with major opera stars throughout his career. He has made audio and video recordings with such artists as Frederica von Stade, Paul Plishka, Maria Ewing, and Edita Gruberova, including a highly acclaimed film of Rossini's *La Cenerentola* produced at La Scala in Milan. Although conducting now occupies most of his time, Desderi continues to be a sought-after performer in companies such as the Rome Opera, where he appeared in a production of Donizetti's *La Fille du Régiment* during their 1998 season. In 1999 Desderi left his post at the Teatro Verdi in Pisa to become the opera director of the Teatro Regio in Turin. Like Andrea, Claudio Desderi is a native of Tuscany. He was born into a musical family in Florence, and throughout his years of traveling has always kept that city as his home base.

Recalling the audition, Desderi said, "When we met each other, he was very serious in his attitude." When rehearsals began, Desderi noticed that Andrea fit in with the cast and crew and showed up every day fully prepared. "He spent one month in rehearsal," Desderi continued, "which is the normal period of rehearsal for a production. His physical situation never changed his attitude, and he just worked with us like everybody else."

Each young artist felt a natural impulse to make Andrea comfortable in music rehearsals; in blocking rehearsals, in which the singers learn where to move on stage; and in the complex maze of the backstage area and among the structures of the opera set. "Obviously, all of us were trying to put him in the best condition to sing," recalled Desderi.

"What I like to remember is really his simplicity and his dedication as a singer, as a musician," he continued. "He was young, he was making a debut in the opera; he was conscious of that. He did everything that was necessary to do and did exactly as everybody else."

Andrea's role demanded emotional expression as well as beautiful singing. *Macbeth* is

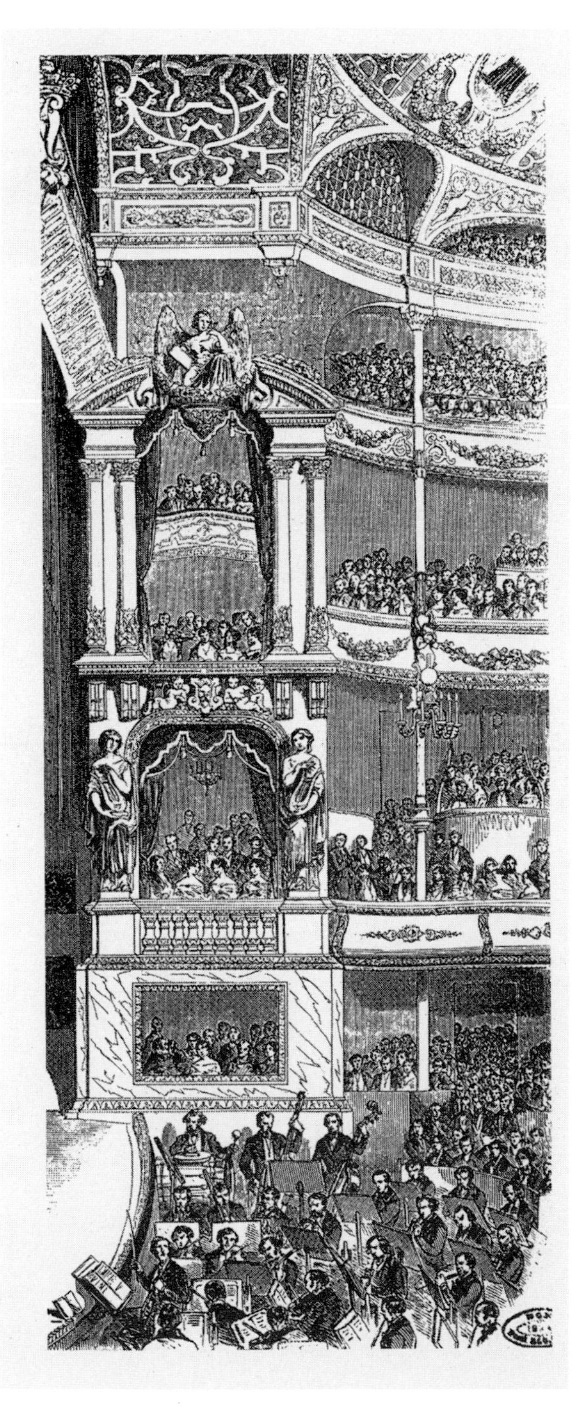

Verdi's first opera based on a drama by Shakespeare, and the composer insisted that the singers who premiered the work put a strong focus on the text. In a letter to soprano Marianna Barbieri-Nini, who would be the first Lady Macbeth, Verdi instructed: "The plot is taken from one of the greatest tragedies the theatre can boast of, and I have tried to . . . write music tied, as far as is possible, to the actual words and the situation. . . . In short, I wish the singers to serve the poet better than they do the composer."

Written when the composer was thirty-four years old, *Macbeth* is Verdi's tenth opera. The dramatic intensity of this opera sets it apart from his earlier work, and it reveals the powerful new inspiration Verdi derived from Shakespeare. *Macbeth* shows, for the first time, Verdi's rare gift for transforming the

This page: Like all European theaters of the nineteenth century, Pisa's Teatro Verdi was designed specifically for the voice. The size of the interior is small enough to allow singers and actors to project perfectly to every section of the theater. Seen from the stage, the horseshoe-shaped, five-tiered theater glows in golden light.

Inset: The dressing room Andrea used during the Macbeth *performances at Teatro Verdi.*

Facing page: Bocelli's first opera performance was in Macbeth *by Giuseppe Verdi, who was revered as an opera composer as well as a national hero. Verdi's name was used as an acronym for "Vittorio Emmanuele, Re d'Italia" (Vittorio Emmanuele, King of Italy) during Italy's movement for freedom and unity in the mid-1800s.*

playwright's passionate and deeply psychological ideas into music. In the drama of *Macbeth,* Verdi was inspired as never before. In a note to his librettist he wrote: "This tragedy is one of the greatest creations of mankind! If we can't make something great with it, let's try at least to make something out of the ordinary." The outstanding acclaim received by the opera in Europe and America proved that they succeeded in creating something extraordinary. In the story, set in eleventh-century Scotland, Macbeth murders King Duncan in an attempt to take over the throne. Once in power, Macbeth and his equally bloodthirsty wife plot to kill one of his generals, Banco (Banquo), and his son in order to prevent them from ever coming to power. Banco is murdered and his son escapes, but Macbeth's tyranny continues to tear the nation apart. In the final act, the nobleman Macduff—the role played by Andrea—kills Macbeth with his sword and becomes the hero of Scotland. For Andrea, making his debut on the opera stage in a Verdi opera was a powerful experience. In Italy, Giuseppe Verdi (1813–1901) is glorified for being much more than one of the greatest opera composers of all time. He is revered as one

Photo: Archives of Antonia Felix

TEATRO DI PISA

Regione Toscana
Presidenza del Consiglio dei Ministri/Dip. generale dello Spettacolo

STAGIONE D'OPERA DELLA TOSCANA 1994

Pisa, Teatro Verdi

sabato 24 settembre, ore 20.30, turno A
domenica 25 settembre, ore 16.30, turno D
lunedì 26 settembre, ore 20.30, turno B
martedì 27 settembre, ore 20.30, turno C

MACBETH

melodramma in quattro parti di Giuseppe Verdi
su libretto di Francesco Maria Piave, dall'omonima tragedia di Shakespeare
edizioni musicali G. Ricordi & C. S.p.A., Milano

personaggi e interpreti (in ord. alfab.)

Macbeth: **ALBERTO MASTROMARINO/ALBERTO RINALDI**
Banco: **ALESSANDRO SVAB/PAOLO WASHINGTON**
Lady Macbeth: **ELIZABETH BYRNE/CATINA FLORIO/PAOLA ROMANÒ**
Dama di Lady Macbeth: **MILENA STORTI**
Macduff: **ANDREA BOCELLI/ANTONELLO PALOMBI**
Malcom: **RICCARDO CARUSO/ALESSANDRO NENCI**
Medico: **ENZO DI MATTEO**
Domestico di Macbeth; Sicario: **DINO MUSIO**

i cantanti si alterneranno nelle diverse recite

Maestro direttore e concertatore: **CLAUDIO DESDERI/MARCO BALDERI** (27 sett.)
Regia: **PATRIZIA GRACIS**
Scene: **GIOVANNI CARLUCCIO** • Costumi: **MASSIMO POLI**
Immagini fotografiche: **MINO LA FRANCA**
Maestro del Coro: **GIAMPAOLO MAZZOLI**
Coreografie: **RAPHAEL BIANCO**

Orchestra: **Camerata Musicale**
Coro **ACA Artisti Coro Associati**
Corpo di ballo: **gruppo allievi dell'Ensemble**, coordinato e diretto da **Marina van Hoecke**

Maestri collaboratori **Lorenza Mazzei, Laura Pasqualetti, Pieralba Soroga** • Maestro alle luci **Francesca Marchesi**
Scenografi realizzatori **Roberta Lazzeri, Beatrice Meoni** • Sculture di **Roberto Grossi**
Assistente alla regia **Matelda Cappelletti**
Direttore di scena **Maria Grazia Martelli** • Assistente alla direzione di scena **Laura Iacopetti**
Direttore degli allestimenti **Piero Benetti** • Disegnatore luci **Riccardo Tonelli**
Capo attrezzista **Luigina Monferini** • Capo sarto **Massimo Poli** • Capo trucco **Paola Gattabrusi** • Acconciature **Fabio Tozzi**
Direttore di produzione **Alda Giannetti** • Assistente di produzione **Laura Bartalini**

Scene realizzate dal **Teatro di Pisa** • Costumi **S'Art di Cecchi, Cecchini, Hegemann,** Firenze
Attrezzeria **Rancati**, Milano • Parrucche **Audello**, Torino • Calzature **Sacchi**, Firenze

NUOVO ALLESTIMENTO • COPRODUZIONE TEATRO DI PISA, CEL TEATRO DI LIVORNO, TEATRO DEL GIGLIO DI LUCCA

per informazioni tel. Teatro di Pisa 050/941.111
i caratteri dei titoli sono stati gentilmente concessi da Nistri Lischi Editore

Archives of Antonia Felix

of the leaders of Italy's move toward independence, a role that he both loved and hated during the turbulent mid-1800s. Not only did he write operas with slightly disguised political messages to rally the Italian national spirit, he also devoted much time to political work. His ability to speak for the collective heart of the Italian people, both as a statesman and as a composer, elevated him to the status of a modern deity in his country. Biographer Charles Osborne describes Verdi as "the greatest and most popular Italian of the nineteenth century." This reputation is alive and well in Italy today,

Above: The program booklet for Andrea's Macbeth *with the Opera Theater of Pisa.*

Facing page: The first time Andrea Bocelli's name appears on an opera poster: the 1994 Macbeth *production at the Verdi Theater in Pisa.*

and all aspiring opera singers with Verdian voices dream of the day they will sing in their first Verdi opera. Franco Corelli, the renowned Italian tenor and one of Andrea's teachers, also performed the role of Macduff during his years with the Metropolitan Opera. The company's general manager, Schuyler Chapin, was surprised when Corelli approached him about singing the role because it's traditionally done by an up-and-coming, relatively unknown tenor. Corelli was one of the biggest opera stars in the world at the time, and one of the Met's most highly prized artists. "I know Macduff is usually sung by a *tenore comprimario*, and I know there is only one big aria, but it is a wonderful role for acting and ensemble singing and I would like to do it," Corelli told Chapin. The general manager wasn't sure Corelli was serious about performing what he considered an "important but modest role," but the tenor assured him that he was. Corelli sang Macduff in a Metropolitan national tour production in Dallas, Texas, to great acclaim. Chapin described his performance as "superb, both vocally and as an actor. When he appeared to announce Duncan's murder, his distress and horror were palpable." For the first time, *Macbeth* was performed with three superstar artists: Sherrill Milnes as Macbeth, Grace Bumbry as Lady Macbeth, and Franco Corelli as Macduff. Dallas audiences enjoyed a history-making event that has not yet been repeated in the opera world.

Even though Macduff does not appear on stage as frequently as the lead roles, the part contains enough drama and beautiful music to allow a good tenor to shine. Macduff's aria, "Ah, la paterna mano," builds to a soaring high A, a hair-raising high note that is still in the comfortable range for any good tenor. The Teatro Verdi production traveled to three other opera theaters in Tuscany, the Teatro del Giglio in Lucca, Teatro la Gran Guardia in Livorno, and Teatro Sociale in Mantua. When Andrea stepped onstage in Lucca, he entered another hallowed place in the world of opera: the theater in which some of Puccini's first compositions were performed, including his second opera, *Edgar*. Lucca is the birthplace of Giacomo Puccini (1858–1924), and his home in the heart of the charming ancient city has been transformed into a museum that is a mecca for opera lovers. Near

Bocelli on stage in the role of Macduff in Macbeth *in September 1994. His teacher and mentor, the renowned tenor Franco Corelli, had performed the role with the Metropolitan Opera and undoubtedly encouraged Andrea to audition for it in Pisa.*

Photo: Teatro Verdi

the Teatro del Giglio is the Church of San Martino, where Puccini was an organist in his youth. Local legend has it that the financially strapped young musician lopped off the top of some of the organ pipes to sell for cash to buy cigarettes. Other famous moments in Teatro del Giglio's history include one of the early performances of Rossini's *William Tell*,

WHEN ANDREA STEPPED ONSTAGE IN LUCCA, HE ENTERED ANOTHER HALLOWED PLACE IN THE WORLD OF OPERA: THE THEATER IN WHICH SOME OF PUCCINI'S FIRST COMPOSITIONS WERE PERFORMED.

and evenings with Verdi and Donizetti as they presided over their own operas. When the company traveled to the Teatro Sociale in Mantua, they entered another city famous in opera history: it was here that the world's very first opera was performed, Claudio Monteverdi's *Orfeo*, in 1607. Andrea's mini-tour with Macbeth swept him through a few of provincial Italy's most historic landmarks.

Word spread throughout Italy that Andrea Bocelli would be on the opera stage in these regional theaters. Fresh from his front-page victory at the San Remo Festival, he was a hot new Italian celebrity when the *Macbeth* production began and it was inevitable that the press would pay special attention to his opera debut. This was wonderful for the company, of course, because the entire production was reviewed by national newspapers that would not otherwise cover regional theater in these towns.

On Bocelli's first night at the Teatro Sociale in Mantua, the crowd was clearly antici-

Top: The production of Macbeth *toured to two other regional theaters, including the Teatro del Giglio in Lucca. One of the historic city's most prized landmarks, this theater is closely associated with Giacomo Puccini, who was born in a house nearby. The Puccini house is now a museum and a popular pilgrimage site for music students and opera lovers.*

Bottom: The interior of the Teatro del Giglio in Lucca, including the dressing room where Andrea prepared for his Macbeth *performance.*

Photos: Susan Turner

pating his entrance onstage. Everyone in the seventeen-hundred-seat, three-tiered theater was curious about how the blind singer would handle himself on the set. One critic in the audience described these rather anxious moments: "The audience was holding its breath at his first entrance when Bocceli/Macduff has to go through a very narrow corridor singing 'Orrore, orrore!' He does this almost running. Another difficult moment was during the supper with the ghost of Banco, when he is lifting his chalice along with the others." Andrea moved securely through it all, with no missteps to report, wrote the critic: "Rehearsal after rehearsal, Bocelli has made the set on stage of the opera his own. . . . The applause was only for him when he sang the aria, 'Ah, la paterna mano' and at the end, from the height of a pedestal, he killed Macbeth."

After the performance, the reviewer asked conductor Desderi about how he communicated with Bocelli from the podium. "Before being a conductor, I have been a singer myself, too," answered Desderi, "and I know one of the problems. When I'm conducting I don't look at my singers in the face, but I look at the mouth of the stomach, here, when they have taken the breath. Bocelli came to me about eight months ago, and his vocal means seemed to me good. Likewise is his instinctive nature for singing. I thought he could succeed. Macduff is a character that does not require special stage exhibitions or risks, and the role of Macduff is a pure character who has never seen the horrors of the world, a little bit like Bocelli."

The review in *Il Tirreno*, headlined A FULL-BLOODED BOCELLI, described the production as one involving "the unexpected success of Andrea Bocelli, who in . . . 'Ah, la paterna mano' has given a rendition with assurance; a version a little bit mannered (with a strong preponderance for inspiring pity) which nevertheless is allowed by the situation summarized in the text. Bocelli was expressive, obtaining personal success in spite of the handicap of his blindness, well overcome in scenes thanks to the solution of the direction, specially done and very discreet." The article closes with the reviewer's portrayal of Bocelli's future, which could go one of two ways: either he would content himself with secondary roles and very modest yet steady salaries, or take the risk of going after a big, rich career in which many stars fade too quickly. "We hope that his heart will decide," the reviewer wrote.

Appearing as Macduff was an exciting challenge for Andrea's debut, and conductor Claudio Desderi recalls that "he did the first performances very well. It was very satisfying, and a good sign for his future."

Andrea recorded his Macduff aria a year later on *Viaggio Italiano*, an album of arias and Neapolitan songs.

Andrea Bocelli is not the first blind tenor to sing on the Italian opera stage. Giuseppe Borgatti (1871–1950) was a tenor star of La Scala, Rome, Genoa, Naples, and international opera houses in the early twentieth century, and also distinguished himself as a powerful Wagnerian tenor in performances at Wagner's Bayreuth Festival. At the age of thirty-six he began to experience the first signs of his illness, glaucoma, which gradually led to his complete blindness in about fifteen years. He then retired from opera but continued to perform in concert. Another tenor who became blind during his career was Vittorio

Lois. Born in 1890, he made his opera debut in 1912 and was renowned as a strong tenor with an "iron voice" and wonderful high notes. Lois sang in many of Italy's major and regional opera houses such as Naples, Verona, Venice, Milan, and Pisa, and continued to sing in opera productions after he became blind in the 1930s. Vittorio Lois is perhaps the only blind tenor to have sung a role in a staged opera before Andrea Bocelli made his debut in Pisa in 1994.

After *Macbeth* Andrea did not appear in another opera for three and one-half years. His skyrocketing concert and recording career had quickly turned him into a globe-trotting performer with little time to learn new roles or devote a full month to rehearsing an opera. In 1988, however, he let the whirlwind stop in order to return to the stage. One of his longest-held dreams had come true. He was offered a chance to sing Rodolfo in *La Bohéme*.

This opportunity came from Mario Dradi, one of the powerful new figures who had come on board to help shape Andrea's career. In addition to being an opera agent who handles stars such as José Carreras, Dradi is one of the world's most successful classical music producers and television moguls. It was Mario Dradi who televised the first Three Tenors concert from Rome in 1990 to an audience of one and one-half billion viewers. Each year it's Mario Dradi who produces the glittering, star-studded, and globally televised "Christmas in Vienna" concert. It's Mario Dradi who creates unique televised events such as a peace concert from Medjugorje, the holy pilgrimage site in Bosnia-Herzegovina, and performances of Mozart's *Requiem* in Sarajevo. And now, it's Mario Dradi who is finding the ideal classical venues for Andrea Bocelli.

Dradi envisioned a *Bohème* that would be televised for RAI, the Italian television network, and licensed to stations throughout the world. The theater in Cagliari, a town of about two hundred thousand on the island of Sardinia, was about the same size as the Teatro Verdi in Pisa where Bocelli sang his first *Macbeth*. Dradi and Bocelli felt that Cagliari was remote enough to deter the hordes of press people who would automatically show up at Italy's main theaters such as those in Rome, Venice, Turin, or Milan. Andrea wanted to use this production to gain more stage experience and tackle the role of Rodolfo for the first time in an out-of-the-way venue. He didn't want to attract the global press. "I was hoping they would not come as far as Cagliari," he said. "I was thinking that maybe I could use this as a practice to pick up the best of what I am able to do, and to live this, my first experience, personally, without intimidation and without having too much said about its merit." He had visited the island of Sardinia several years before in search of horses to buy. He found the horses beautiful, but they were beyond his budget at the time.

The stage director whom Mario Dradi chose for this *Bohème* was the internationally acclaimed Lorenzo Mariani, a young American who had worked in major opera houses in both Europe and the United States. A native New Yorker, Mariani studied theater at music at Harvard and then art and theater history in Florence on a Fulbright scholarship. He apprenticed with opera directors such as Franco Zeffirelli, Luca Ronconi, and Jean-Pierre Ponnelle before directing his own productions in Paris, Barcelona, Tel Aviv, Rome, Bologna, Parma, Turin, Florence, Monte Carlo, Geneva, Chicago, and Tokyo. Mariani's

Italian-American parents own Asti, a restaurant in New York City, and now that Lorenzo and Andrea are friends, the tenor and his entourage can be found relaxing and eating there when they are in town.

With the theater chosen, a cast lined up, and the stage director hired, Dradi had one part of the puzzle yet to complete—hiring the conductor. He knew which maestro would be perfect for the job, a young American on his own roster named Steven Mercurio.

For three years Mercurio had conducted Dradi's "Christmas in Vienna," and the producer was well aware of the conductor's strengths in performance situations that required some extra effort, such as working with a singer with little stage experience. Mercurio had conducted pop-rock singer Michael Bolton in a "Christmas in Vienna" concert as well as that singer's classical album, *My Secret Passion*. His likable, down-to-earth rapport with orchestra musicians, opera divas, and pop singers alike gave him an extra edge to meet the unique challenges of this *Bohème*. Dradi needed someone who could firmly connect with an inexperienced opera singer who would never be able to see his baton. He was determined to get Mercurio for the job, and persisted when the conductor told him he was already scheduled to do a *Tosca* for Opera Pacific in the United States at that time.

Steven Mercurio's career has brought him to the podium of opera houses in cities throughout the world, including Rome, Monte Carlo, Brussels, London, Amsterdam, Bonn, Seattle, Philadelphia, Dallas, and San Francisco. For five years he was the music director of the Spoleto Festival, the annual summer extravaganza of music, dance, drama, and art launched in 1977 by his friend, composer Gian Carlo Menotti. Mercurio's high-

Conductor/composer Steven Mercurio, a young New Yorker with a distinguished international career and the conductor of Andrea Bocelli's La Bohème *in Cagliari. He went on to direct Andrea's first American tour with the Pittsburgh Symphony as well as many other performances. Andrea's inability to see him on the podium is not a problem, he explains, because the most important communication between a conductor and a singer on stage is not visual.*

Recalling the Bohème *rehearsals and performances, Mercurio said, "With Andrea I made sure that I was able to read his body or was able to read when he took that breath. In great opera you feel each other."*

Photo © J. Henry Fair/CAMI

profile American positions have included that of principal conductor of the Opera Company of Philadelphia, assistant conductor at the Metropolitan Opera and associate conductor of the Brooklyn Philharmonic. In the tradition of American musicians like Leonard Bernstein, Mercurio is also a composer. His work includes a highly respected finale to Puccini's last, unfinished opera, *Turandot*. Mercurio arranged several of the pieces played by the Pittsburgh Symphony on Bocelli's U.S. tour, and created new arrangements for the album *Sacred Arias*. An *Opera News* profile described him as a conductor with "solid musicianship, relentless drive and nervy confidence" who is "poised to become our next star composer-conductor."

When the producer kept calling Mercurio to ask that he free up his schedule to do this *Bohème,* Mercurio finally asked, "Why do you need *me* to do this?" Dradi gave him a full description of the production and of its main attraction, Andrea Bocelli, the blind Italian tenor who was topping the pop charts throughout Europe. "Basically," Mercurio said, "they wanted me because I had done a lot of *Bohèmes*; I was the music director at the Spoleto Festival for five years in Italy, so I speak Italian; I can deal with the Italian orchestras, and especially in a situation like this. They knew that I had the patience to deal with a situation that might need a little attention, a little patience." The conductor admitted that he hadn't heard of Bocelli, so Dradi sent him a copy of the "Con te partirò" duet with Sarah Brightman. Suddenly Mercurio recognized the voice and the recording: someone had sent it to him when he was preparing for Sarah Brightman's appearance in "Christmas in Vienna." He recalled being curious about "the Italian guy" that was singing the duet with her in the recording. With the CD in his hands a second time, he made the connection. At home in New York after he had decided to do *Bohème* and successfully gotten out of his *Tosca* contract, Mercurio turned on Channel Thirteen one night to see Bocelli in *A Night in Tuscany*. The video was playing constantly for the station's major-league blitz of a holiday fund drive. "That's the guy!" he recalled yelling at the television. " 'That's the guy I'm supposed to do this *Bohème* with two months from now!' That's when I finally saw who it was. And then they sent me *Romanza,* so I got an idea of what I was going to deal with."

In January 1998, everyone assembled in Cagliari to begin putting the opera together. Puccini's *La Bohème* is considered by many to be the perfect opera. Puccini created six characters, two young women and four men, that people of any age or culture can relate to. Drawing partly upon his experiences as a conservatory student in Milan, Puccini recalled the atmosphere of a city lightly shaken up by the fresh ideas of the Scapigliature, or bohemians. He set his opera in Paris, where a much more lively and earthy bohemian phase had inspired Henri Murger's popular book, *Scènes de la vie de bohème*. With a genius for melody, for crafting sounds that evoke precise emotions, and for weaving a tight-knit drama in which not a moment of music or action is wasted, Puccini wrote what many believe is the opera of operas. From shy hints of falling in love to rowdy lovers' quarrels to intimate loss, *La Bohème* celebrates light and dark aspects of real life without overcomplicating the characters or the music.

Rodolfo, the lead tenor role played by Andrea, is a poet who lives in the Latin Quarter near his equally poor yet happy friends Marcello, a painter; Schaunard, a musician; and Colline, a philosopher. In the first act, Mimì, a neighbor, knocks on the door and asks Rodolfo for a match to relight her candle. When she drops her key, they both kneel on the floor to look for it, but their candles go out. In the dark, Rodolfo takes Mimì's hand and begins to sing the delicate aria "Che gelida manina." *What a frozen little hand, let me warm it . . .*

Mimì then describes her humble life to Rodolfo in "Mi chiamano Mimì" ("They call me Mimì"). As they reveal themselves to each other, Rodolfo falls in love with the shy, frail, and beautiful little seamstress who has so suddenly and unexpectedly stepped into his life. She tells him that she is ill, and he hears it in her cough. The conversation goes

Puccini's La Bohème *has been one of Andrea's favorite operas since he was a child. He viewed his first performance as Rodolfo in the 1998 production in Cagliari as a personal challenge to determine whether or not he could meet all the physical demands of this—or any—leading opera role. His success meant he was victorious in the most difficult challenge of his musical life. "Being onstage means pulling down barriers seemingly insurmountable," he said. "I demonstrated my knowledge of how to move on stage. I demolished a barrier."*

Photo © Agenzia ANSA

deeper and the act closes with a duet in which Mimì and Rodolfo declare their love.

Act II is a twenty-minute romp set at the Café Momus on Christmas Eve. Marcello's girlfriend, Musetta, is dining with a wealthy admirer because she and Marcello have quarreled. Rodolfo arrives and introduces Mimì to his friends, and Musetta makes up with Marcello. In Act III, Rodolfo and Mimì express the joys and difficulties of their love over the past few months. Mimì's consumption has gotten worse, and in addition to her failing health she is disturbed by Rodolfo's terrible jealousy. It appears that this love is too much for both of them and it may be best to part. They agree, however, to stay together until the spring. In the final act, Mimì is brought to Rodolfo and Marcello's attic apartment so weak and ill that she cannot stand. As her friends run out to sell their possessions to buy her medicine, her condition worsens. Finally, when she and Rodolfo are alone, Mimì tells him how much she loves him and dies in his arms. Rodolfo cries out her name . . .

Luciano Pavarotti considers Rodolfo his favorite role. "I identify so much with Rodolfo," he once wrote in an essay for an encyclopedia on opera. "He is an artist and he is a romantic, and, although he is supposed to be French, by the time Puccini got through with him he became totally Italian. Above all, he is una persona viva—a true, living person—and that is why I never tire of playing him. His feelings are my own. . . . Like all good plays, *Bohème* is like a wound-up spring: once it starts unwinding, nothing can stop it. . . . That is not true of many operas."

La Bohème, Puccini's fourth opera, was to be followed by such masterpieces as *Tosca, Madama Butterfly,* and *Turandot.* The composer's unshakable determination to become an opera composer—a successful and great opera composer, in fact—came to him one night in his youth. Even though he had inherited the talent of five generations of musicians, Puccini wasn't very motivated in his studies. He grew up singing in the choir, playing the organ, and playing the piano in some of Lucca's darker neighborhoods to make extra money. By the time he was a teenager he knew he didn't want to be poor for the rest of his life, but he wasn't excited about the prospects of teaching or being a church musician. One day Puccini heard that Verdi's *Aida* was being performed in Pisa, about fifteen miles away. He had played through and marveled over some of the master's scores but had never attended a performance of one of the operas. He spent his last cent buying a ticket—which meant he had to walk the fifteen miles to Pisa to see the show. It was a good investment (for all of us), because the performance changed his life. Walking home through the hilly countryside in the middle of the night, the eighteen-year-old knew that he would write operas. No choral music, concertos, symphonies, or piano studies—only music for the lyric stage. He felt in his bones that he would be the next great opera composer to succeed Verdi. He later said, "When I heard *Aida* in Pisa, I felt that a musical window had opened for me. Almighty God touched me with his little finger and told me to write for the theater—mind, only the theater." With this burning new desire and sharp focus, he threw himself into his studies and eventually attained the top of his class at the conservatory in Milan. With the very important support of career-making or -breaking music publisher Giulio Ricordi, Puccini did become the rightful heir to Verdi.

Photo: Archives of Antonia Felix

Giacomo Puccini composed La Bohème, *his fourth opera, over a period of three years. He was born in Lucca and lived his entire adult life in a country villa in nearby Torre del Lago. Bocelli was born just a few miles south of Lucca and has always been affected by the atmosphere of Puccini that is so prevalent there. "Towards Puccini I have a profound connection," he said. "We breathed the same air, as if we breathed the same joy, the same sweet sadness in the fog that I have breathed."*

Puccini wrote slowly, producing only twelve operas in forty years. *La Bohème* was completed at midnight on December 10, 1895, three years after it was begun. When he laid down his pencil, he was so moved by the death of Mimì that he burst into tears. "Standing in the middle of the study," he later wrote, "alone in the silence of the night, I began to weep like a child. It was as though I had seen my own child die."

By the time he arrived in Cagliari for rehearsals, Andrea had memorized his role. Actually he had learned the first-act aria years before and been performing it on his concert tours. Andrea has listened to and loved *La Bohème* since childhood and, like Pavarotti and countless other tenors, he identifies with the character of Rodolfo. "I feel like in reality he and I actually resemble each other in a certain number of ways," he said. "There is the spirituality of the man but also something about the physical aspect, and I think one does a better job when you feel you have some familiarity with the character." Andrea grew up near Puccini's birthplace, Lucca, as well as the nearby village of Torre del Lago where Puccini spent his adult life. This close proximity has given Andrea a strong affinity for the composer. With the sentiment of a romantic poet, he once described his feelings for living on Puccini's *terra sacra*: "Puccini, to me, seemed someone that I would love, like he would be a friend, not a far-distant historical person. We breathed the same air, as if we breathed the same joy, the same sweet sadness in the fog that I have breathed. It's as if we flowered with the same water, we saw the same scenery, shared the same solitude—the emptiness and the fullness of life. So towards Puccini I have a profound connection. Thanks to him, when I was a little boy I was able to imagine. I studied, and I put every-

ANDREA GREW UP NEAR PUCCINI'S BIRTHPLACE, LUCCA, AS WELL AS THE NEARBY VILLAGE OF TORRE DEL LAGO WHERE PUCCINI SPENT HIS ADULT LIFE. THIS CLOSE PROXIMITY HAS GIVEN ANDREA A STRONG AFFINITY FOR THE COMPOSER.

thing I had into becoming Rodolfo."

Andrea's weeks of preparation were nerve-wracking and exhausting. His contract stated that he had to arrive in Cagliari on January 21 and rehearse eight hours a day for the four and one-half weeks before the premiere on February 18. In the course of those rehearsals he suffered from insomnia, was overcome with anxiety, and lost more than fifteen pounds (seven kilos). Performing in concert throughout the world had never taken such a toll on his nerves, nor had he ever lost an ounce on a tour. He felt the importance of the event on his entire being.

The decision to do the opera had not come quickly, because he knew what a colossal task he would be undertaking. "I was called to be in this part, and I tried very hard to think before I accepted it," he said. "And I took time to accept it. My legs were trembling just at the idea of singing the most beautiful opera in the world to me. But this was big for me; this *Bohème* was the appointment with my destiny. It was something that I could not miss, even if it scared me to the extreme. If I had pulled back, what kind of artist could I call myself? How can I call myself an artist and not face this challenge? I had to face it and be brave against this and conquer my fears continuously. This also serves me for my own condition, to demonstrate to myself that I can do these things even with my handicap." *La Bohème* gave Andrea the chance to finally test himself on an issue that had haunted him for years— as a blind person would he be able to perform in a staged production? "I grew up as a child with this music," he said during the rehearsal period. "I always had it in my blood. There was a period I realistically thought it impossible for me, because of my sight problem, to overcome the obstacles present in this style of music. Then . . . at a certain point, I . . . went headlong into it."

Andrea's sense of this operatic initiation went beyond the question of whether or not he would sing well. His performance would be a living statement of his ability to reach a new level as a performer and as a human being. If his family had been very supportive of him throughout his childhood and school years, there were some teachers in his life who insisted on throwing cold water on his dreams in the name of being "realistic." His mother recalls one very tough high school teacher who *faceva la guerra*—would make war—with her son. She didn't learn about it until later, because Andrea kept these battles to himself. The message Andrea received from authority figures such as this teacher are deeply embedded. "It was said," he recalled, "very clearly, and with fairness, 'You can do many things, but you cannot become a tenor. You cannot follow the conductor, you cannot go onstage, you cannot do that. Direct yourself elsewhere.' " The pressure of this belief bore down upon him while he prepared for *Bohème*. Personally, there was so much at stake. "Being onstage means pulling down barriers seemingly insurmountable," he said one day during the third week of rehearsals.

Working out the stage movements would take longer than usual because Andrea needed time to memorize every inch of the set. Stage director Lorenzo Mariani didn't water down any of the action for the leading man's role. "I didn't do anything at all to make it easier for him," he said. Movements that had to be repeated again and again until they were graceful and spontaneous looking included dancing, jumping, running toward Mimì, placing her down and picking her up from a bed, turning on cue, ripping up a manuscript and throwing it in a stove, lighting the stove, sticking a cigar in someone's mouth, and more. The stage director was pleased. "Everyone remains perplexed when I tell them that during the rehearsals Bocelli was moving onstage with perfect ease," said Mariani. "He had his own technique for understanding the stage, in five minutes he could catch every detail. He did everything needed of Rodolfo, from setting the table to dancing a minuet with Marcello, to gathering Mimì in his arms and laying her down gently on the bed."

Any tenor singing Rodolfo for the very first time faces a huge task. The focus of the entire opera is on him and Mimì, and he appears in every scene except the very opening of Act III. One of Puccini's best-known characters, he undergoes a wide range of experiences and emotions in the drama, from playfulness to jealousy to grief. Conductor Steven Mercurio recalled that Andrea had to spend about twice as much time as the average tenor to build this character in relation to the other actors and learn the staging. "There were a lot of factors with this," Mercurio said. "First of all, you can never forget the fact that he was inexperienced. Even if he were a sighted person, if it were anyone in the world doing

On stage in La Bohème *with Italian diva Daniela Dessì as Mimì. "I felt great tenderness from Andrea," she said. "We had to do a lot of rehearsal, but he is a very sharp man and has great musical instincts." Andrea was very enriched, musically and intellectually, by the intense four-week rehearsal process in which he felt privileged to work with world-class musicians such as Dessì.*

Photo © Agenzia ANSA

their first Rodolfo, it would already be a traumatic experience. Let's just get that straight. The fact that he had so little stage experience, sighted or not, is already difficult. The fact that he's in the public eye as much as he is, so that every little burp that came out of his mouth would be criticized, was already too much pressure; then the fact that he can't see meant that he needed twice as much time to get used to the environment."

Andrea knew that his theater inexperience was going to pose the most problems for him vocally, which is why he hoped Cagliari would be more of a testing ground for him. In addition to acting and stage movement, a major part of the training for opera singers is learning how to deal with the acoustics of singing in the theater. It's a completely different technique than singing in the studio or singing with microphone amplification. "When you deal with a studio singer," said Mercurio, "they're so used to being amplified and using monitors. In his concerts he gets to hear the orchestra at whatever volume he wants and he gets to hear his own voice at whatever volume he wants. When you stand onstage and suddenly sing full voice, you don't hear the orchestra that well anymore. A sound that you're used to hearing at the piano suddenly becomes a clarinet line that fades into the woodwork. Instead of a bass on the piano which is always so loud, the orchestra, in the pit, doesn't feel like that. It's much more transparent. It will take a long time to adjust to a natural acoustical balance. Your voice just doesn't come back. You sing out into the theater and none of it's coming back to you—you feel you're just singing to a void. That's real life."

Andrea's musicality would also be put to the test—not only in his interpretation of the score, but in his timing and musical entrances. He would not have the benefit of glancing quickly to the pit from time to time to catch a cue from the conductor. According to Mercurio, this was not a problem. He's adamant that the most important communication between the singer and the conductor is not visual. "Without her glasses, Maria Callas couldn't see five fingers in front of her face," he said. "So what did she do? It's called: 'We rehearse.' Andrea and I rehearsed a lot together so that there were no surprises. No, I don't just accompany him from the pit. No good opera conductor should just be following the singer. It's a rapport that changes from beat to beat. If he needs a little more time, I give it to him. If he's getting himself in trouble, I'm going to start to move him through it and he'll hear it and start to respond. He knows that I know him, so he trusts that I will guide the performance in his best interest. I also know that if he makes a mistake it's my job to cover it up. That's why you rehearse. You rehearse to come to as much of an understanding as you can, to develop the same breathing and feeling of the music.

"Ultimately, the bottom line is that if somebody's musical, they're musical. If they're musical and they have it in their body, it's not that tough to accompany or to work with them. It just isn't. Too much is being made over whether somebody can follow the conductor visually. In great opera, you feel each other. Yes, there might be an attack here, where you look at the conductor. In those moments with Andrea I made sure that I was able to read his body or was able to read when he took that breath. I can feel when he's trying to push out the end of a phrase, and he can feel when I've got the orchestra making a crescendo that's pushing him to a certain point and he's going to arrive. There's no substitute for musicality. The fact that he can't see only means that we have to work a little harder and that he can't do things in a capricious way; that we have to make decisions. We have to understand each other more, depend on each other more. I've had tenors who can see look right at me and make more mistakes than he made in that *Bohème*! They look right at me and they're still making mistakes, because they're picking up the light in their eyes, or their makeup is running down their face, or the soprano got in the way. There are so many things that can distract. You just rehearse to get over those."

The star of *Bohème* is Mimì, played in this production by soprano Daniela Dessì. Andrea had sung a duet from *Bohème* with Dessì the previous year in a benefit concert at the Vatican. This Genoa-born diva, managed by Pavarotti's agent, Herbert Breslin, has sung Mimì more than sixty times in theaters throughout the world. Her other Puccini heroines include Tosca and Butterfly, and she is renowned for her Verdi heroines such as Desdemona in *Otello,* frequently sung with Plácido Domingo; Elisabetta in *Don Carlo,* which she has sung at La Scala with Pavarotti; Alice Ford in *Falstaff*; Violetta in *La Traviata*; Leonora in *Il Trovatore,* and the title role of *Aïda*. She made her Metropolitan Opera debut in 1995 as Nedda in Leoncavallo's *I Pagliacci,* and debuted with the San Francisco Opera as Donna Elvira in Mozart's *Don Giovanni*. She has made several recordings of full operas including a *La Bohème* for EMI, *Don Carlo* for EMI, *Falstaff* for Sony, and a *Pagliacci* conducted by Riccardo Muti for Philips, as well as a disk of Verdi and Puccini arias for Forlane. Cast with Daniela Dessì, Andrea had the benefit of a costar with enormous experience, someone who knew the opera intimately and would do everything possible to help him shine.

Photo: Herbert H. Breslin, Inc.

Soprano Daniela Dessì, a native of Genoa, is renowned throughout the world for her Puccini and Verdi heroines. She has sung in many of the world's major opera houses including La Scala, the Rome Opera, Zurich Opera, Metropolitan Opera, and Lyric Opera of Chicago with such stars as Luciano Pavarotti and Plácido Domingo. Before singing Mimì opposite Bocelli's Rodolfo in La Bohème, *she had sung the role more than sixty times, which gave her an intimate knowledge of the opera that she generously shared with her costar.*

> "IF THAT *BOHÈME* DIDN'T MOVE AS SMOOTHLY AS IT DID, HE'D NEVER EVEN BE ATTEMPTING THIS AGAIN THE REST OF HIS LIFE."
> —*Conductor Steven Mercurio*

Steven Mercurio was moved by Daniela's gracious demeanor with Andrea. Day after day he witnessed her patience and extremely supportive attitude. Not every world-class diva would take the extra time or expend the extra energy to help a novice who was already getting more publicity for the show than she. "Daniela is at the top of her game," he said. "She's at the Met, La Scala; she's done the role and is at the prime of her career. She was very kind to Andrea. She was very careful in duets with him not to blow him off the stage; she always tried to match him when they were doing duets. She was very kind to him because she knew what was at stake. She had the ability, like I did, to either help him or destroy him. If that *Bohème* didn't move as smoothly as it did, he'd never even be attempting this again the rest of his life. That's my opinion. A lot of it had to do with Daniela's grace. She was a very good colleague to him on and off stage. Often the press totally ignored her, saying, 'get out of my way, I'm talking to Bocelli,' while she's a *diva*! She had to put up with an awful lot, which I give her a lot of credit for."

Andrea also expressed great admiration for his costar. "Dessì is an extraordinary partner. I don't have to talk about her vocal prowess, because she's wonderful. But her humanity . . . she is an extraordinary colleague."

"I felt great tenderness from Andrea," said Dessì after the first performance. "He did something miraculous. I assisted him with great affection." Like everyone, she was surprised at Andrea's facility on stage. "His actions onstage were very believable," she said. "We had to do a lot of rehearsal, but he is a very sharp man and has great musical instincts. During one rehearsal, I made a move that hadn't been staged, and I worried that when he started to walk toward me he would go into the orchestra pit. So I took a big, sharp breath to indicate where I was. He said, 'Good. Now I will always know exactly where you are.' "

The day before the opening, Andrea received flowers and cards offering good wishes from dozens of friends including Luciano Pavarotti, Plácido Domingo, Zucchero, and his teacher and mentor, Franco Corelli. When he arrived at the theater the next day, Enrica and their two sons came along and settled into his dressing room. Enrica had been with him during every rehearsal, bringing an atmosphere of peacefulness and calm that soothed his nerves and helped him maintain his sanity.

Any hopes that the press would stay away from out-of-the-way Sardinia were crushed by the afternoon of the premiere. The streets and parking areas near the Teatro Lirico were dotted with television vans and cars that had delivered the troops of reporters and critics. Mario Dradi and Andrea's carefully wrought plan to keep this production out of reach of the global press had failed. Andrea was painfully aware of their presence. "Everybody came, and I may not have seen them, but I could perceive their stares." He sensed the tension in the audience before his first act aria and each of his main musical entrances. He felt that half of the audience was there to cheer him on and the other half was anxiously awaiting a mistake, a reason to bring him down. "Maybe for this reason," Andrea said, "my son Amos, who is only three years old, held me tight in between one act and another, and when

I came back to the dressing room, he did not want to leave me anymore, and he said, 'Papa, don't go back out there.' He was crying and telling me that I should stay back and not go back out there. I felt in peril, it was a great strain for me, my suffering, and he intuitively was able to pick up on that with the acuteness that only a child is capable of."

The tenor's family provided a strong focus for his energy and helped him stay grounded in what he had to do. His was so nervous that at some points in the evening he worried that he might not be able to go back on. But then he would think about the people closest to him, the ones who would love him no matter what happened, and he regained his perspective. "I held on to Amos very tightly," he said, "and my second son, Matteo, who is only four months old, was sleeping in his little crib. They were my strength, my children and my wife, Enrica, and with them I waited for the last part of the scene. Everything else that happened, really I did for the three of them. With their fear for me, it was hard for me to go back into the role, because I had to be 'hard' to go back into the role, [but] with them I found tenderness and it brought out in me what I needed."

When the final curtain came down, Andrea was hit with an emotional storm of both relief and exhilaration. His colleagues were full of praise, and he was quite satisfied. Steven Mercurio was thrilled that Andrea had not only survived in such nerve-wracking circumstances but had done very well. "He worked hard, he studied hard, and it was a success," the conductor said. "When it airs on television, people will see that the whole cast was very, very good. The orchestra played well. We had a great time." However, the conductor knew that Andrea felt bad about some of the reviews. He took the singer aside and went to great lengths to explain to him what the reviewers did—and did not—criticize. "Certain critics wanted to beat him up on the fact that his technique wasn't really a stage technique yet, and some of them just resented the fact that he was making an awful lot of money and he was famous, and how dare he? There was a lot of moralizing going on, just like there is now about his *Werther* in Detroit. People who have never seen or heard him have already decided whether he should or should not be doing it. That's the cross he's got to bear for being rich and popular.

"The response was so mixed," continued Mercurio. "Every person who walked in already had an agenda, a predisposed idea. On a general note they were amazed that he actually did the staging and survived. He didn't make gross mistakes, he didn't go walking into the orchestra pit, he moved better onstage, much better, than anyone had imagined. No one had to walk him around. He did everything he was asked to do. I think everybody, whether they wanted to like him or not, was impressed with the fact that he did move; it didn't become a negative theater experience because he wasn't able to see. He did everything that was required of the role. I think everybody respected that. Clearly, the real big opera people knew that he was not going to come in and be Corelli, that his voice was not going to have that projection. Those who love him and wanted to be there to see him do it had a great time. Those who wanted to be skeptical and cynical had their turn, too."

In his straightforward, rapid-fire New York style, Mercurio continued to describe the review coverage of this important moment in Andrea's career and how it affected the singer. "Andrea was always hurt by the reviews," he said, "by the people who didn't like him vocally. I sat down with Andrea and said, 'Let's examine what they said. They didn't say that you didn't know the piece, that you didn't sing the piece, that you didn't move onstage; they didn't say anything about your performance. All they could say was that your vocal technique is not that of Luciano Pavarotti, which you know to be the truth. So where's the big criticism? Where's the big problem here?' I tried to tell him to look at the critics and understand what was really said. They didn't say anything about the text, didn't say anything about whether he was correct or that his intonation was horrible—they said he wasn't loud! So what? Kathy Battle wasn't loud. Cecilia Bartoli isn't loud. 'And you know this,' I told Andrea, 'so work on it. Big deal.' "

If he was disturbed by some of the reviews, Andrea was also deeply pleased over his own achievement. He had set himself up for a *prova del fuoco,* a trial by fire that would test his psychological, emotional, and musical limits, and in this he knew he was victorious. In the next day's *Corriere della Sera,* he was quoted as saying, "I'm emotional, but happy and above all very satisfied. I demonstrated my knowledge of how to move onstage. I demolished a barrier."

Only Andrea knows how wide and tall this barrier had been.

Exactly one year after flexing his theater muscles in *Bohème,* Andrea entered the studio to record the opera with Zubin Mehta and the Israel Philharmonic. Immersing himself in *Bohème* once again was wonderful, but he looked forward to being onstage in another opera. He enjoyed the challenge of learning a new role and missed the experience of interacting with other singers during an intense rehearsal period, something he had found very stimulating and enriching in Cagliari. A tight schedule of concerts and recording kept him out of the opera world, however, until the summer of 1999, when he was scheduled to perform in Franz Lehár's operetta *The Merry Widow*. The show would be staged at the Arena di Verona, with Andrea making his operetta debut in the leading role of Count Danilo Danilovitch.

The Merry Widow is lighthearted musical theater, Viennese style. Filled with glorious waltzes, it dates from 1905 and is Lehár's most famous operetta. Other famous comic operas from Vienna include *Die Fledermaus* by Johann "the Waltz King" Strauss, a favorite in opera houses everywhere during the New Year's season. In England, this mid-nineteenth-century style took the form of Gilbert and Sullivan's clever and lively comic operas, such as *H.M.S. Pinafore* and *The Pirates of Penzance*, and in France light opera was the domain of composer Jacques Offenbach, who created popular hits like *La Belle Hélène* and *The Tales of Hoffmann*. Unlike the comic opera of Gilbert and Sullivan, Viennese operetta such as *The Merry Widow* calls for more operatic voices, and the dialogue that appears between musical numbers is spoken instead of sung.

Operetta would be a fresh and unusual new theater experience for Andrea. The lighthearted and bubbly *Merry Widow* opens with a sparkling Parisian ball scene, and this production would include a large choir and dance troupe, the first stage appearance of beloved Italian television personality Fabrizio Frizzi, a state-of-the-art light and mirrors show, and two giant screens that spelled out the libretto for everyone in the huge amphitheater to see. As Count Danilo, Andrea would be the handsome and commanding leading man who, by the end of show, gets the girl.

The Arena di Verona is one of the world's most dramatic places to experience opera. The third largest amphitheater in the world, it was built in 30 A.D. and it gives concertgoers the thrill of sitting on the same stone benches as the ancient Romans who flocked there to watch gory mock battles and gladiator fights. In the Middle Ages the Arena was the place of choice for noblemen who challenged each other to duels, and later it was the setting for bullfights, tournaments, and theater. The circular shape of the stone walls gives the amphitheater perfect acoustics, making it one of the most popular places to view operas with extravagant sets, such as Verdi's *Aida*. Many singers have been overwhelmed by the size of the Arena the first time they stand upon the stage. Accommodating 16,600 spectators, it is about 502 feet (152 meters) long by 422 feet (128 meters) wide and 99 feet (30 meters) high. One feels like a tiny toy with no hope of sending the voice across the impossibly vast space to the opposite end of the stadium. But looks are deceiving. Voices carry beautifully in the open-air theater due to the resonance and echo effect when the sound hits the stone walls. The Arena carries a unique tradition that is played out during every evening performance. At dusk, everyone in the audience lights a candle. The curved rows outlining the circular theater and the straight rows of seats in front of the stage become bathed in candlelight, a stunning effect for the audience as well as the performers.

Promising a sell-out run packed with adoring Bocelli fans from all over Europe, *The*

Merry Widow would be the highlight of the summer entertainment season. Unfortunately, Andrea was still in a hospital bed in Munich when rehearsals began. He was flattened by a sudden attack of sciatica in his back. By the fourth week of June, the producers had to face the fact that they would probably have to replace Andrea with another tenor because he just wouldn't have enough time to rehearse.

On June 28 Andrea still hadn't been able to provide a certificate from his doctor that he was well enough to begin rehearsing, so the company hired someone else for Danilo. The show must go on, figured Veronese Foundation supervisor Renzo Giacchierri, but it can't go on without Andrea. The production team put their heads together and came up with a compromise. Andrea was sure to be back on his feet by mid-July, when the show opened. Knowing that operetta can work with all types of unconventional effects (which you can never get away with in grand opera), they whipped up a spiffy new attraction in Act II. During the party scene, a woman in the cast announces that her friend, an Italian opera singer named Andrea, is about to arrive. The crowd, who had been disappointed that Andrea didn't appear as Count Danilo, begins to go wild, and pandemonium breaks loose when Andrea rolls onto the stage seated in an elegant vintage car. He exits the open convertible and sings "La donna è mobile" from Verdi's *Rigoletto,* then the Neapolitan song "La Brindisi." The crowd's wild standing ovations brought the show to a standstill after both pieces. Bocelli had performed in his first operetta after all, and everyone was thrilled with the results, from the producers to the cast to Bocelli's fans to the star himself.

He may not have been playing the Count, but after all of his performances Andrea, as

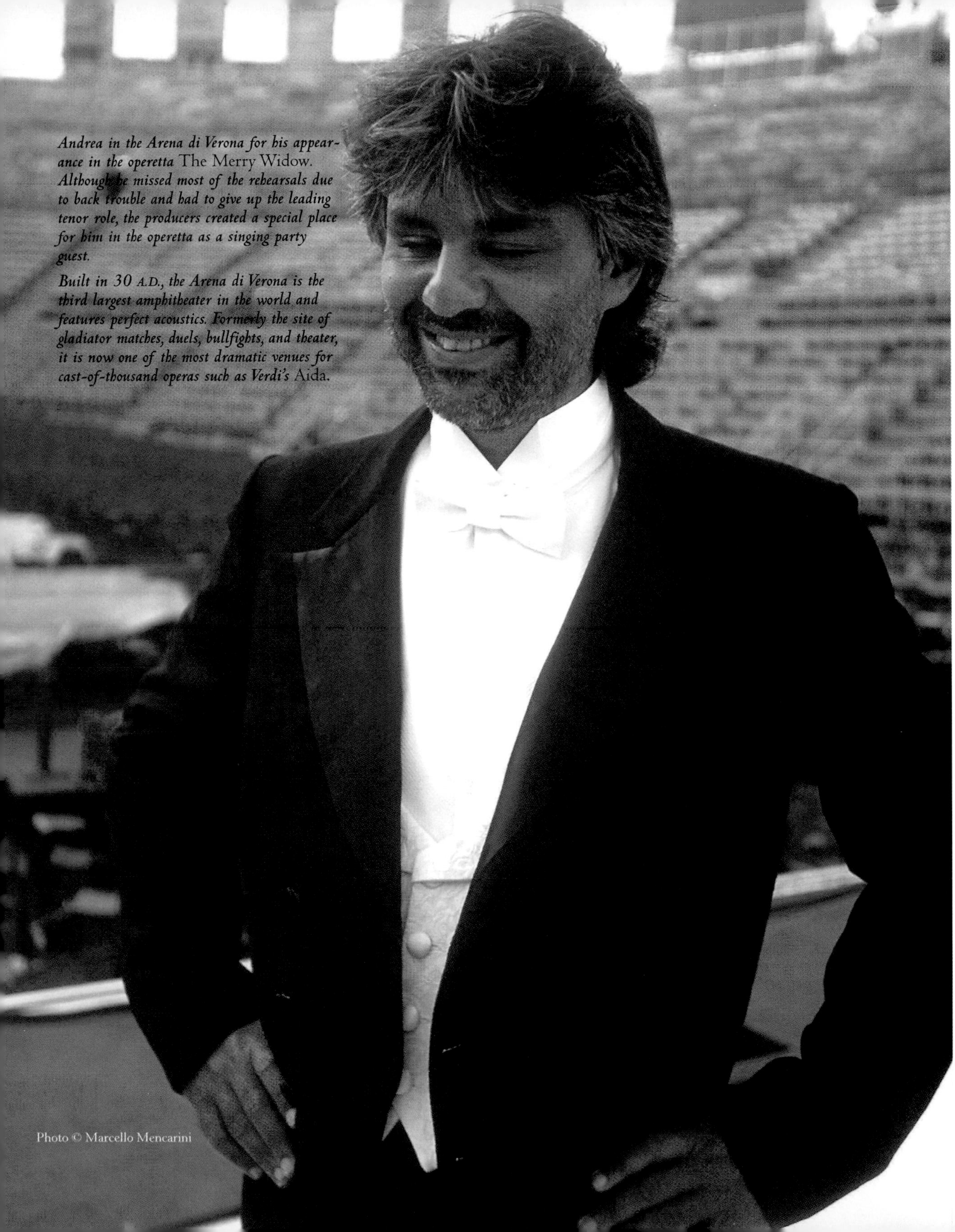

Andrea in the Arena di Verona for his appearance in the operetta The Merry Widow. *Although he missed most of the rehearsals due to back trouble and had to give up the leading tenor role, the producers created a special place for him in the operetta as a singing party guest.*

Built in 30 A.D.*, the Arena di Verona is the third largest amphitheater in the world and features perfect acoustics. Formerly the site of gladiator matches, duels, bullfights, and theater, it is now one of the most dramatic venues for cast-of-thousand operas such as Verdi's* Aida.

Photo © Marcello Mencarini

usual, was met backstage by his family—and got his girl.

Andrea's third serious opera is also to be his debut on the American opera stage. He will sing the title role in Massenet's *Werther* for Detroit's Michigan Opera Theater (MOT), one of the most distinguished opera companies in the United States, in the autumn of 1999 (after this book has gone to press). For years Andrea had been saying that his popularity as a pop singer is his vehicle for getting a shot at opera. Nowhere is this more true than in the story of how he got his role in Detroit.

After the first of Andrea's two very successful concerts in Montreal in July 1998, conductor Steven Mercurio got on the phone to describe the event to David DiChiera. "You've got to come up here and see this!" he told him, knowing that DiChiera—director of a major American opera house—and Bocelli—a tenor with a huge draw—each had something to offer the other. Mercurio was convinced that if DiChiera could see the amazing effect Bocelli had on an audience, bringing ten thousand people to their feet with screams usually reserved for a Rolling Stones concert, he might be interested in talking to the tenor about singing

FOR YEARS ANDREA HAD BEEN SAYING THAT HIS POPULARITY AS A POP SINGER IS HIS VEHICLE FOR GETTING A SHOT AT OPERA. NOWHERE IS THIS MORE TRUE THAN IN THE STORY OF HOW HE GOT HIS ROLE IN DETROIT.

with his opera company. Bocelli's popular album *Romanza* drew his fans to these sold-out concerts, and the fans' enthusiastic response to the singer performing opera arias caught the attention of David DiChiera.

Mercurio has worked frequently with David DiChiera, conducting operas for him at both Opera Pacific and the Michigan Opera Theater. The training program that David DiChiera developed with his Michigan Opera Theater has launched the careers of several American opera stars, including Kathleen Battle, Leona Mitchell, and Catherine Malfitano, and under his leadership MOT has become one of the nation's major opera companies. DiChiera is enormously committed to building the careers of young singers. On Steven Mercurio's recommendation, he was looking forward to hearing and meeting Andrea Bocelli.

Photo: Courtesy Michigan Opera Theater

David DiChiera, general director of the Michigan Opera Theater. Andrea Bocelli will make his America opera debut with this company in the autumn of 1999 singing the lead role in Massenet's Werther. *Dr. DiChiera has received many letters from Bocelli fans throughout the United States expressing how Bocelli has introduced them to the world of opera. The director describes Bocelli as "an exciting artist, with a tremendous amount of charisma," and says, "I hope his presence will mean that people who are not operagoers will be tempted to come into our opera house."*

DiChiera flew up to Montreal for Bocelli's final concert. He had never seen anything like it. "The crowd was absolutely wild with enthusiasm," he recalled in an interview in July 1999. "It was fascinating to me. I just brought the Three Tenors to Detroit, and this was the same kind of thing. There are certain artists in the world of opera over which the audience just becomes hysteric in their response. These singers, like Andrea Bocelli and the Three Tenors, are able to touch something indefinable in the audience that makes them react in a very emotional and excited way."

As he listened to the concert, DiChiera was certain Andrea would sound beautiful in his opera house. He began to think about which opera roles would work well with his voice. "I was very impressed with the beauty of the voice," he said, "primarily the way in which he is able to communicate directly to the listener. When we're in the business of opera, we tend to immediately analyze and dissect the voices, figuring out whether it's lyric or spinto or leggero and all those classifications. But when I listened to Bocelli I felt that the unique thing about him, the quality that explains in part why he has such a huge following, is his ability to communicate directly to the listener. They are very touched by it. I was also very impressed with the range of his voice, particularly the upper register. His high notes are exciting; he has the ability to sustain them, to give the right excitement in the right places at the climax of a piece. There are many tenors who probably have had more operatic experience than Bocelli but who, when it comes to those 'money notes,' it's not a thrill. Those two things combined make him an exciting artist, plus the fact that he's an attractive man who has a certain charisma about him."

David DiChiera stayed in Montreal for a few days to meet with Andrea and his management. He also had some private conversations with the singer and learned about his aspirations and goals. "I enjoyed him because there's a tremendous directness about him and a nice warmth," said DiChiera. "His enthusiasm for opera really came through. You can tell that his desire to express and to communicate in music is through opera."

IN THE DISCUSSIONS ABOUT WHICH OPERA WOULD BE IDEAL FOR ANDREA'S AMERICAN PREMIER, A FEW IDEAS WERE TOSSED AROUND. THE GROUP FINALLY DECIDED UPON *WERTHER*.

In the discussions about which opera would be ideal for Andrea's American premier, a few ideas were tossed around. The group finally decided upon *Werther.* "When Andrea said he'd like to do *Werther*, I thought it the ideal role," said DiChiera. "I could easily imagine him as the romantic, introverted poet who gives his life for an unrequited love. I think it's a role that will be very, very successful for him."

One of the most popular romantic French romantic operas, *Werther* is the eighth opera by Jules Massenet (1842–1912). Among the composer's other twenty-six operas, the most successful are *Manon, Thaïs, Hérodiade,* and *Le Roi de Lahore*. The story is based on a literary masterpiece of the previous century, Goethe's *The Sorrows of Young Werther*. This novel, written in the form of a series of letters from Werther to his friend, Wilhelm, creates a detailed portrait of an extremely sensitive and deep-feeling young poet hopelessly in love with a young woman who does not return his feelings. Even after Charlotte marries her fiancé, Albert, Werther relentlessly pursues her. After one last refusal, Werther borrows Albert's pistols, returns to his room, and shoots himself in the head. Charlotte rushes to his house, finds him near death, and finally reveals that she has loved him all along. Werther asks her to have him buried in his favorite corner of the graveyard, and his final thoughts are of one day meeting her in heaven. Rather than bemoaning his death, he says that his life is just beginning: *Vois, je ne crains plus rien! You see, I am not at all afraid!*

In the Michigan Opera Theater production, Andrea's costar will be Denyce Graves, an American mezzo-soprano whom he greatly admires. The role of Albert will be sung by Christopher Schaldenbrand, a baritone who has also recorded the role. "In the meeting in Montreal Andrea was very thrilled that Denyce Graves is going to be Charlotte," said DiChiera. "I told him that I would do everything I could to make this happen, and I did. Christopher Schaldenbrand is a very talented young baritone and I'm particularly excited about him because he's from Detroit. I think this production is going to give him a really fine homecoming."

Mario Coradi from Milan will be the stage director of *Werther,* and David DiChiera has made special rehearsal arrangements that will give Andrea much more time onstage with the sets. "I made the decision," said DiChiera, "that in order to give Andrea the kind of support and structure he needed, I had to provide a rehearsal period that was completely onstage, with the set in place for each scene. That's never what we ordinarily do. I felt that we needed to provide this for him so he would have the chance to familiarize himself completely with the physical layout of the sets from the very beginning. Normally singers

Photo: Courtesy Michigan Opera Theater

rehearse with tape on the floor to signify certain pieces of furniture, etc., but that's not a viable alternative here. Since the opera company is one of the few in the country that actually owns its own opera house, this is something I can control and make available for him. Most opera companies rent the facility from civic auditoriums and their rehearsal time is often limited."

The Detroit Opera house is one of the largest in the country, with twenty-seven hundred seats. DiChiera is certain that Andrea's voice will do well in the theater's acoustics. "It's a very singer-friendly opera house," said DiChiera. "Singing here will be very positive for him; this is a house where singers project very easily. It's beautifully designed; the depth is relatively short, so the whole audience is quite present and available to the stage. I think it's an ideal house for Andrea."

David DiChiera hopes that this collaboration will be the beginning of an ongoing professional relationship with Andrea Bocelli. He is happy to be one of the guides in the tenor's early operatic career. "I've always been interested in promoting careers; it's what makes my job very exciting for me," said DiChiera. "Even though Bocelli is world

The interior of the Detroit Opera House, which has twenty-seven hundred seats. For Andrea Bocelli's United States opera debut, general director David DiChiera believes that the theater will be filled with Bocelli fans, many of whom have never before been to an opera; Detroit's regular operagoers; and directors of other American opera companies who are curious about Bocelli's vocal projection and stage ability in the opera house.

Photo: Courtesy Michigan Opera Theater

famous, I feel I have taken a role in promoting his operatic career, and I find that very satisfying. Being successful on the opera stage is not only about experience, it's also about having a certain conviction and projecting. When I hear someone sing, I ask myself, How would that work in this opera or that? I've always felt that this is my responsibility and greatest pleasure, identifying singers and hoping to promote and build their careers.

Hopefully this will be just the beginning for us, but I believe that a lot of my colleagues will be here for *Werther* to hear Bocelli, too. There will be a number of them who at this point didn't feel comfortable taking the risk. For me, it has been a pleasure to work out something that would enhance what Bocelli's goals are."

Since word began to spread that Andrea Bocelli would sing in Detroit in the autumn of 1999, the opera house has received a lot of mail from fans requesting tickets and expressing their excitement about attending Andrea's American opera debut. David DiChiera has been inundated with letters from people who have never been to the opera before, but are more than willing to check it out if Andrea Bocelli is going to be in the production. He has also received letters from handicapped people who wish to thank him for bringing even more popularity to Bocelli, who is bringing new inspiration to their lives. "They're very committed fans and audience people," he said. "I've had letters from people who are handicapped who say that they are so proud of Bocelli because he has demonstrated that nobody need be in a position where they cannot fulfill their dreams, regardless of what they may have to overcome. And a lot of people just write to say thank you so much for bringing him to the opera house."

La
Voce
5

The voice is a mystery," said tenor Franco Corelli. "You can form the voice, mold it, to a certain point, but not beyond. You can take Caruso's records and imitate his voice. But you can not go against your own nature too long. . . . Technique does not come only from thinking about making a sweet, beautiful note. You must also think sweet *with* the technique. These things are tied together." These remarks by Corelli are in Jerome Hines's collection of interviews *Great Singers on Great Singing*. One of the great voices of this century, Corelli began to teach after retiring from the stage and is energetically giving master classes today at the age of seventy-six. Andrea Bocelli met his idol at a master class in Turin, but he considers himself a lifelong student of the tenor because has been listening to his recordings since he was a child. He received his first Corelli recording from his *tata*, nanny, and "immediately fell in love with the voice that has a thousand qualities . . . full of force, of life, a river of a voice. [His] voice had this property to be extremely communicative, so that it entered directly into my heart at that time.

"My studies with Corelli were quite brief," Bocelli continued. "I attended his master class in Turin and had a few classes at home with him. But even today, there is a confidence between us. And if I am studying some songs, I will call him and go over them with him on the telephone. But, in a way, Corelli was always my coach. His voice got to me and was the one I wanted to emulate. When I began to work out songs, they were his songs. It was by listening to his recordings that I acquired a notion of how to sing."

Andrea first heard Corelli sing at a Puccini Festival concert he attended when he was still in school. Hearing the legendary tenor live was an experience he still carries with him. "What impressed me was the same things that had impressed me from the record," he said. "The way of projecting sincerity, intensity, which is singular to Corelli. Even if I have encountered this repeatedly, and I have met Corelli many times now and we have this human simpatico . . . I feel within me always a great emotion. An anxiety almost."

Andrea Bocelli's voice study began late, in his thirties. Although he took group voice lessons in junior high school in Bologna, he did not begin serious technical study until he was much older. When he made the decision to quit the law and devote himself to singing, he began to study with Luciano Bettarini, a teacher from Prato, northwest of Florence. "He's a very old man," said Bocelli. "He worked before with many, many big tenors like Beniamino Gigli, Tagliavini, Del Monaco, Corelli—big experience. For two or three years I went three times each week." Then Andrea attended the master class with Corelli and took a few private lessons with him afterward. He recalled the day he stood by the piano and sang "Che gelida manina" from *La Bohème* in Corelli's class. "At the end, big silence," said Andrea with a laugh. "He was very close to me, with his hands on my shoulders, and he told me, 'Very good.' "

[BOCELLI] HAS A GREAT WILL. HE ALSO HAS A HEAD THAT WORKS VERY, VERY WELL. HE IS TRULY A VERY INTELLIGENT PERSON WHO HAS MADE HIMSELF NINETY PERCENT ALONE."
—*Franco Corelli*

In an interview broadcast on Italian television in November, 1998, Franco Corelli talked about Andrea's potential. "I think that Bocelli has every right to study the opera," he said. "Why not? It is logical that Bocelli today finds himself a little difficulty in singing opera, not the difficulty in how to carry an aria to the end, but how he gives up the foundation of the voice, in a certain sense, to sing the little songs [doesn't support his voice well when he sings popular music]. If he throws himself into opera, he can obtain better results in a few months . . . because he has got the quality. He has a great will. He also has a head that works very, very well. He is truly a very intelligent person who has made himself ninety percent alone, which shows that his head works very well.

"Today he has to bring to an end this singing of songs," Corelli continued, "owed principally to a microphone. One must pass from the microphone to the theater." Corelli, whom Bocelli admires for having such a distinctive quality, believes that Bocelli has a special sound that distinguishes him, too. "He reminds me of the wonderful Tuscan voices," said Corelli. "I'm speaking of color; it resembles Bastianini, Marzianini, these voices. It is a little like this quality and is very beautiful." In general, Corelli feels that Andrea hasn't yet settled into his voice completely, hasn't given himself over to it in a way that allows him to make the operatic roles his own. " He is sometimes a bit—I am not saying introverted—but still restricted a bit," said Corelli. "He doesn't let himself go enough. But when he succeeds in giving himself completely, then things will be even more beautiful, surely."

Photo: Metropolitan Opera Archives

Franco Corelli, one of the great voices of the century. Andrea Bocelli participated in one of Corelli's voice workshops and took a few private lessons with the renowned tenor. A powerful singer with movie-star looks, Corelli was the Metropolitan Opera's biggest star in the sixties and seventies, singing 263 performances with the company. Bocelli heard Corelli on a recording when he was a child, and "immediately fell in love with the voice that . . . entered directly into my heart."

Bocelli describes Franco Corelli as "a very sweet man, very kind." He is also very fond of Luciano Pavarotti, with whom he spent a week talking about voice technique and the opera world at the tenor's home in Modena. Pavarotti had invited Bocelli to be his guest before performing in his "Pavarotti and Friends" concert in 1994. "Maestro Pavarotti, he too gave me very, very important suggestions," said Bocelli. "I've been one week in his home. I remember we spoke so much about the technique in general, and he told me always, 'Remember to speak soft' [without pressure on the throat], and this is very important because I think that this is the first: to sing like we speak."

With the generosity for which Pavarotti is famous, he offered Bocelli tips on singing as well as a veteran's insights on the nature of the business he was getting into. "I received some very important lessons, technically," said Andrea. "It was very important to have this moment with him. He gave me much advice and treated me like a father to a son. . . . He is also someone who is extremely straightforward. . . . He always encouraged me although it is true that he asked me: 'Why do you want to bother with opera? It is a difficult and monopolizing world.' " When Bocelli and his pianist/voice coach Carlo Bernini arrived at the house, Pavarotti made every effort to make them feel at home. "It was all done in a very natural way," said Andrea. "I got to his house, he welcomed me sitting at a table piled with cakes and desserts, like Father Christmas. We ate together and then very naturally moved into another room, where there was a piano. So my accompanist found himself with me on one side and Pavarotti on the other. He was a bit intimidated by this." Between the shop talk Pavarotti and Bocelli discussed horses and Pavarotti indulged his protégé as an honored house guest. "I remember the plates of pasta that would be brought to me in the garden!" Andrea said. Bocelli now refers to Pavarotti as "Maestro," and feels indebted to him for his generosity as both a musician and a human being. "He has always been extremely good to me," said Andrea, "maybe too much. I will try to prove my gratitude to him forever."

In between concert appearances and studio time, Andrea works on opera roles by studying the braille scores. His old friend and piano teacher, Carlo Bernini, has become his primary coach and musical assistant on all his projects. Carlo had heard Andrea in piano bars around Pisa and only knew of him as a lounge pianist. He had no idea that the singer had serious musical aspirations. When Andrea first approached him to take piano lessons from him, Carlo had to be convinced. "He didn't want me!" Andrea recalled jokingly in a television interview with Carlo at his side. "I asked to study the piano with him, because I had interrupted my studies some years ago. He judged me undisciplined and little inclined [for serious lessons]." Carlo did accept Andrea as a student, however, and the two became great friends. As Andrea's career began to develop, he depended on Carlo to help him work on the arias he recorded and sang in concert.

Steven Mercurio has worked extensively with Carlo Bernini as a vital link between himself and Andrea, as in rehearsals for the *La Bohème* production in Italy. "Carlo Bernini was the rehearsal coach for Andrea in Cagliari," Mercurio said. "He was there the whole time. When we did the tour last summer [in the United States], Carlo went with us the whole time. Carlo is Andrea's official coach. He's very helpful because when there's something to be fixed, if Andrea's making the same mistake two or three times, I just turn to Carlo and say, 'fix that. Get on that.' Carlo is a good assistant to have around because he bulldogs the problems and can stay on Bocelli to make the constant corrections." He adds that Carlo will accompany Andrea to Detroit to work with him in all the rehearsals for *Werther*. Carlo's official job will be as Mercurio's assistant. "Carlo is Andrea's only full-time coach. For all the music that Andrea learns, Carlo is sitting at the piano playing every note, 'bing bing bing.' "

Carlo Bernini set up a study discipline for Andrea in which the singer vocalizes and sings two hours a day. He accompanies him at the piano in recital and has been at his side on every tour. Having been familiar with Bocelli since he was a complete unknown, Bernini is in a unique position to see how the singer has handled his fame. "I always knew him as an exceptional young man," Carlo said. "For me he has stayed the Andrea I knew fifteen years ago."

In addition to working on his music with Carlo Bernini, Andrea also takes voice lessons from a young teacher named Maurizio Agostini in Italy. When time permits and he is home for a period of weeks, he sets up lessons with Agostini to work on technique. A very disciplined person, Bocelli always takes braille music with him on trips and works with his coach on the road. "I spend a lot of time in airplanes, and after all,

Bocelli in recital with Carlo Bernini at the piano. Bernini is Andrea's longtime friend and voice coach, accompanying him on every tour and for every performance. They met in the 1980s when Bocelli sought Bernini out to take piano lessons from him. Now, Bernini is instrumental in helping Andrea learn new songs and opera roles.

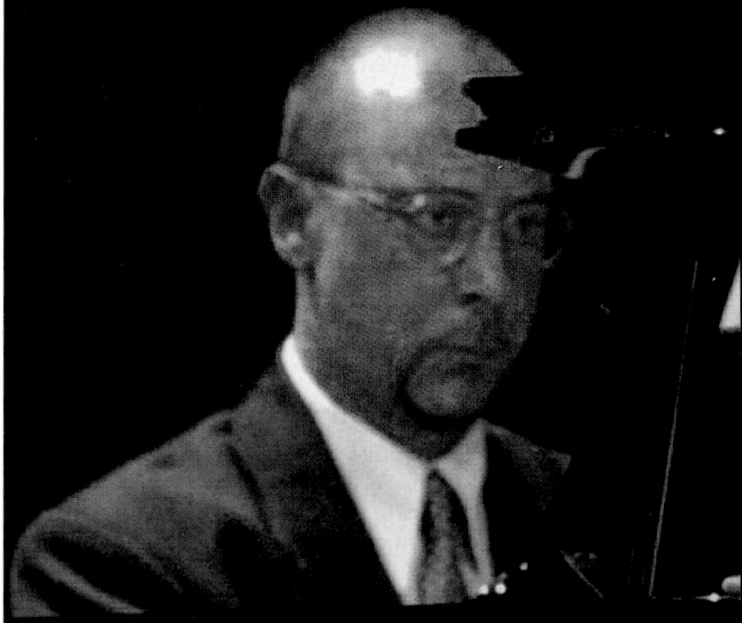

in the towns I am not able to do any sightseeing," he said. "So I try to fill the leisure time with voice lessons and exercise."

One of the aspects of professional singing that plagues Bocelli as well as many other singers is stage fright. Even some of the most experienced stars of opera struggle constantly with nerves, as was certainly the case for Corelli. The singer was notorious for canceling performances due to fear of failure and an overwhelming anxiety about facing the audience. An opera singer of his generation tells the story of Corelli's wife, Loretta, hovering about backstage during Corelli's performances at the Met, calling out to him to bolster his confidence, "Franco, you're beautiful! Everything is going perfectly! You're beautiful!" As the story goes, stagehands had to take her back to Corelli's dressing room because she could be heard in the audience. Corelli's stage fright is perplexing to everyone who heard him because he appeared and sounded completely in command onstage—a stunning man with movie-star looks and a powerfully beautiful voice to match.

Much before Corelli's time, Caruso also suffered from terrible stage fright. Pacing around backstage, puffing on the Egyptian cigarettes he smoked every day, he considered the theater a battlefield in which he fought to win over the audience every night. In her biography *Caruso,* the tenor's widow, Dorothy Caruso, wrote, "He was always extremely nervous and didn't try to conceal it. He himself said: 'Of course I am nervous. Each time I sing I feel there is someone waiting to destroy me, and I must fight like a bull to hold my own. The artist who boasts he is never nervous is not an artist—he is a liar or a fool.'"

Pavarotti also admits that stage fright is ever present in his career, regardless of how many times he's performed the role or how good his voice feels. He too is convinced that fear is an integral part of the business of singing—it keeps the singer on his or her toes. "Although confidence is important for a young singer," he wrote in his autobiography, "I also believe it is important not to be too confident. In fact, in my opinion it is good to be constantly scared. In my own career, I am always nervous, no matter what I am doing. Fear can be healthy if it does not cripple you. The main reason my father did not have a career with his beautiful voice is that he could never conquer the fear." With brutal honesty, the "supertenor" admits that he never feels secure about performing. "People think that because I can go out and sing in front of huge crowds, I must have terrific confidence. I don't. I have bravery, and that is different from confidence. I am always afraid. In fact, I think the only way to be continually successful is to be a little scared all the time. If you are not scared, it means you think something is easy. If you think something is easy, you won't work as hard and you will not be as good as you can be."

"PEOPLE THINK THAT BECAUSE I CAN GO OUT AND SING IN FRONT OF HUGE CROWDS, I MUST HAVE TERRIFIC CONFIDENCE. I DON'T. I HAVE BRAVERY, AND THAT IS DIFFERENT FROM CONFIDENCE. I AM ALWAYS AFRAID." *—Luciano Pavarotti*

In this respect, Andrea Bocelli is conforming to Pavarotti's advice perfectly. "My greatest problem is a psychological one because I really have terrible stage fright," he said. "It takes away my strength. When I go onstage this anxiety decreases somewhat, but it

Photo © Franco Silvi

doesn't go away entirely until the last song." For him, one of the most difficult aspects of singing in concert is trying to find something to do with his hands. Usually he wears a silk scarf around his neck and holds it by the edges. If he doesn't have this prop, his hands wander and distract the audience from his performance. Bocelli is keenly aware that this is not a problem in an opera performance, because the singer has a role to interpret and specific gestures to perform. When performing in *Macbeth* and *La Bohème* he never concerned himself with how to manage his hands; he engrossed himself in the role and let the text and the stage directing guide his movements.

Although the environment is completely different, going on the theater stage to perform opera and walking out in front of an orchestra before a stadium crowd are equally nerve-wracking for Bocelli. "I'm shy," he said. "Everyone knows that I am always very afraid when I go on the stage. . . . There is only one thing that helps: to go onstage and sing."

Lorenzo Malfatti, a colleague of conductor Claudio Desderi, heard Bocelli sing during the *Macbeth* dress rehearsals in Pisa. Now professor emeritus at the University of Cincinnati's College-Conservatory of Music, Malfatti was raised in Italy, attended the St. Cecilia Conservatory and Academy in Rome, and had a long career as a baritone in opera houses throughout the world. He's currently the associate artistic director of the Opera Theater of Lucca, a summer program that gives young students a chance to perform full-length operas at the Teatro del Giglio in Puccini's home town. In his distinguished university teaching career, Malfatti has taught several nonsighted students. Observing Bocelli on the stage of the Teatro Verdi that day made him recall the interesting challenges of working with this type of student. In his experience, the actual technical work was exactly the same as with sighted singers. Once the blind singers learned their

Photo: Susan Turner

Lorenzo Malfatti, associate artistic director of the Opera Theater of Lucca and professor emeritus at the University of Cincinnati's College-Conservatory of Music. Malfatti attended one of Bocelli's Macbeth *rehearsals in Pisa and recalled the unique challenges of teaching nonsighted voice students.*

parts with their braille scores, they were able to work on the music just like everyone else. However, an aspect of singing that had to be addressed with these students more than with sighted singers was the elasticity of the face and not letting gravity pull the expression downward. "The lifting of the facial muscles gives the face life," he said. "The nonsighted students who have been blind since birth have no idea what an expressive face looks like. This was always a very important issue in my studio. I believe that every coach that works with them has to give them expression." Malfatti was impressed with Bocelli's voice and heard great potential in it. He was also enthusiastic about the effect that the tenor's success will have on other singers who are nonsighted. "I think his greatest days are yet to come," he said, "and I wish him well. Bocelli will open up the door for many people, not just the blind, but anyone who has obstacles to overcome."

Bocelli is aware that singing for the opera theater means learning how to project the voice. The size of the voice is not the issue; rather, it is a matter of learning how to make the voice carry through the opera house. "Continuous performance in the theater is fundamental for the development of the voice," he said. Unlike Corelli, whose is classified in the Italian system of voices as a spinto, or dramatic tenor, Bocelli has a light, more lyric tenor voice. The heart of operatic vocal training, for both large and small voices, is in learning how to make the voice resonate and project. Even though he has little experience on the opera stage, Bocelli is committed to his training and is constantly working on his technique. With the continued support of people like David DiChiera, who is willing to carve out more rehearsal time for him onstage, he will have the opportunity to solidify this technique.

Most opera singers gain stage experience early in their training when there is little at stake, unlike Bocelli who, in spite of all attempts to keep the production on a small scale, sang his first leading role under the scrutiny of the entire European press. William Riley, a New York voice teacher with a client list that looks like a who's who of American opera as well as popular music, discussed this issue of stage experience. "The skeptic would say that Bocelli's not going to have an easy time in the big theaters," he said. "All of us who have been through the process of going through life preparing for careers have experiences that are sometimes great and sometimes horrible. For most of us, those rudimentary experiences were done when people weren't looking at us so hard. For him, the world is going to be looking on him with the question of, Is he or isn't he? And that's really not fair. The thing that all of us go through is to sing in progressively larger venues; we sing in universities, we sing in schools, we do workshops here and there. We sing small parts and we have many opportunities to get feedback on whether we're a success or not and what we have to do to make ourselves more successful. In this situation, Bocelli is taking roles in the biggest venues at the beginning."

Riley went on to describe the compelling differences between just singing beautifully—or singing with a microphone—and singing in the theater. "If you're accustomed to singing for the big theater, you're used to planting your sound out there and it goes all the way," he said. "At times you make a sound that is a bit gruff, even as a beautiful lyric soprano you have to make a sound that's going to possess the noise to cut, and I don't mean just tone, I mean those little chips of noise which are not even perceived as such in the audience. We make lots of noises to try to propel our voices into the theater and to have discrimination and character and all those things. Because he has only performed in a couple of operas, I don't think that Bocelli has had the opportunity to learn those lessons yet. Many of us have to learn those lessons the hard way. I remember as a student I worked in a university with a rather large theater of about seventeen hundred seats. I wanted to sing beautifully in my first performance, so I did what I thought was a beautiful job. My teachers, all in turn, came to me after the performance and said, 'Remember, this is opera.' I loved singing songs, and to me song and opera were the same. But they aren't. And it took me a while to learn that if the audience couldn't hear me, they wouldn't *want* to hear me, regardless of what I had to offer."

As voice teacher to Celine Dion, one of Bocelli's friends and biggest admirers, William Riley has watched Bocelli's career with interest. Based on the tenor's live Grammies television appearance in early 1999 (in which Bocelli performed a duet with Dion as well as a solo number), Riley was encouraged that Bocelli is on track in his training. "In the aria he was just breathtaking in his control," Riley said, "and he is a far better singer now than he was three years ago. So obviously he's studying, and studying well."

In the summer 1999 production of *The Merry Widow* performed in the vast outdoor Arena di Verona, Bocelli held his own just fine without a microphone. David DiChiera has complete faith in him for the *Werther* performances in his large theater, where microphones are never used. True to his nature, Bocelli is serious about his training while keeping a healthy sense of humor about it all. "Self-derision is very important for an artist if he wants to move forward," he said. "Someone thinking of himself too seriously does not have the necessary critical distance." Even when the pressure is on, as in a recording studio session when time is money, Bocelli keeps his perspective and rolls with the punches. "I still remember the laughter invading me when I realized that I was completely off track," he recalled about one session. "What made me laugh is that I was thinking it was impossible that I was the funny man singing on the tape."

No one told Bocelli that forging an opera career would be easy, and he doesn't expect it to be. "Everything in this world is hard; every type of objective that we achieve is hard. Where there is competition, there is work. This doesn't frighten me; the main point is to try to improve day by day." He finds it torturous to listen to his recordings because by the time they are released he has made improvements in his singing that were not there when the recording was made. Realistic about the work that still needs to be done on his technique, Bocelli is annoyed by labels given him, such as "the Fourth Tenor" and by comparisons made between himself and Pavarotti and other star tenors. "I don't think I am anywhere near ready to take their place," he said. "I have a million problems. I am in a constant

"ONE DAY HE TOLD A GROUP OF US, 'I HAD A CHANCE TO BECOME KNOWN DOING MY RECORDINGS, BUT WHAT REALLY INTERESTS ME IS EVERY DAY TO LEARN MORE, TO POLISH MY CRAFT, TO DO THINGS OF REAL ARTISTIC VALUE AND INTEGRITY.' "
—Ana Maria Martinez

struggle with my voice. The more I learn technique, the less I know. . . . My voice is undoubtedly a gift from God, but like every gift it must be exercised. It is very communicative, but it is full of defects that must be corrected."

Soprano Ana Maria Martinez, who has sung extensively with Bocelli on his concert tours, observed the singer's daily schedule and his attitude toward his training. "He works so hard," she said. "On the tours he worked every day on his voice. He's always doing exercises. Sometimes we even vocalized together. He's always curious to see what someone else is doing vocally and technique-wise. He also has great integrity. One day he told a group of us, 'I had a chance to become known doing my recordings, but what really interests me is every day to learn more, to polish my craft, to do things of real artistic value and integrity.' "

The tenor's objective is to instill everything he does with genuine emotion. "One has to have love inside to express one's feelings through music," he said. "To find the connection between all the songs that I sing and my own emotions that I put into my voice—this is the only way to do what I do." His mother, Edi, looks at her son's success in simpler terms. "There is a saying in our parts," she said, "'You don't tell a good horse to trot, he gets up and trots on his own.' If Andrea did not have the voice he would not have been able to attain it."

In his journey into the world of opera singing, Andrea has found the most satisfying challenge and deepest mode of expression he knows. "My world isn't dark," he explained. "Standing on the stage to sing, I see the world with my heart."

The Piazza dei Cavalieri, where Bocelli: A Night in Tuscany *was filmed. This famous piazza is just a few blocks away from the law school Andrea had attended twenty years previously.*

Photo: Susan Turner

PBS ROMANCES AMERICA

When Andrea Bocelli signed up with the independent Italian record label Sugar in the early 1990s, no one foresaw the success that was to come—albums and singles staying for weeks at number one and multiple titles on the U.S. *Billboard* charts at one time. Sugar records and Andrea Bocelli have become very wealthy through their licensing agreement with PolyGram, the world's largest record company (until it was sold to Seagram in December, 1998, and became part of a new entity called Universal Music Group). One of PolyGram's biggest and smartest moves with their intriguing "crossover" artist from Italy was to enter the U.S. market through the Public Broadcasting Service, PBS.

Andrea Bocelli got a slow start at PolyGram. Sugar records had to do a lot of persistent follow-up work to make the company take Bocelli seriously. "Even Sugar Music has a problem getting the right attention for the majors," said Filippo Sugar, Caterina's son.

"It took us eighteen months of working with [PolyGram] on Andrea Bocelli before he became a priority for them." Since the success of Bocelli and other "regional" acts, such as Viennese violinist/showman André Rieu, PolyGram has chosen to make this type of artist not only a priority but a cornerstone of their business. Alain Levy, then CEO of PolyGram, learned that carefully selected European artists like Bocelli who are big hits in their own region can achieve success on the global level, too. "The future will belong to the companies which develop artists locally and regionally . . . and eventually break them on a worldwide basis," he said in early 1998. Amazingly, as they found with Bocelli, the "regional" appeal in the United States is so great that foreign language isn't even a problem. Millions of Americans have fallen in love with *Romanza, Sogno,* and Bocelli's other albums without understanding a word of Italian. In 1996, no PolyGram record sold more than five million copies. In 1997, Bocelli's *Romanza* blew that apart by selling nearly seven million copies in that year alone. The album, Bocelli's breakthrough release in the United States, has sold about thirteen million copies to date.

To coincide with the international release of *Romanza* in 1997, the executives at PolyGram in Europe and America put their heads together to come up with a plan for bringing Andrea to the biggest—yet very targeted—American audience possible. Costa Pilvachi, president of Philips (one of PolyGram's classical labels), sent a Bocelli CD to U.S. executive Lisa Altman. She called him back and said, "Costa, I can sell this, this is fantastic, you've got to get this—but we need PBS." She wanted to bring Andrea Bocelli to the same market that had opened its arms to the Three Tenors. The man who could make it possible was the same man who had brought the Three Tenors to public TV, David Horn of Channel Thirteen in New York City. As director of music programming for this PBS station, David Horn had done no less than give the nation a classical music booster shot with the wildly popular Three Tenors show. Once they had an agreement that PBS would air a Bocelli video during the December 1997 pledge campaign, PolyGram went to work producing *Bocelli: A Night in Tuscany*.

"MOST SHOWS FIND THEIR FUND-RAISING VALUE DECREASING AFTER THEY GET SEEN ONCE," EXPLAINED DAVID HORN MORE THAN A YEAR AFTER *A NIGHT IN TUSCANY* WAS FIRST SHOWN. "THIS ONE MADE MORE MONEY AS STATIONS KEPT SHOWING IT. IT HASN'T STOPPED YET."

Complete with light show and dreamy interlude footage of Bocelli on horseback, *A Night in Tuscany* was shot as a live concert in the Piazza dei Cavalieri in Pisa. The stage and seating were set up just a few blocks away from the law school where Andrea, a couple of decades earlier, had been a classics-crazy scholar going after a practical career with a briefcase. David Horn accompanied the production team in Italy, and he describes another element of the video that PolyGram never brought up. "Originally I thought that [Bocelli's] blindness would be perceived as a gimmick," he says. "But my premise was that this guy was selling romance, and because he's blind, he has a certain vulnerability. So we went to Italy, we put him in an environment, we did some packaging." The marketing talk comes off a little rough, but the finished product is neither gimmicky nor sentimental. The video is a tasteful combination of big production and intimate portrait that thoroughly won over the audience. Within three weeks *Romanza* went gold, and the PBS stations that aired the video for their pledge drives made record numbers. "Most shows find their fund-raising value decreasing after they get seen once," explained David Horn more than a year after *A Night in Tuscany* was first shown. "This one made more money as stations kept showing it. It hasn't stopped yet."

PolyGram's strategy for bringing Andrea Bocelli to American audiences can be viewed as a smooth and sophisticated nineties version of Pavarotti's "packaging" as a "supertenor." Pavarotti's manager, Herbert Breslin, has often been criticized for dragging the tenor (and the art form he represents) from the lofty world of opera into commercialism. On the other hand, many hail him for introducing classical music to millions who would not have discovered it otherwise. Regardless of opinion, the American opera world has survived and, it is widely believed, gained enormously from Pavarotti's superstardom. Breslin's marketing savvy, coupled with the big vision of promoter Tibor Rudas, created a new category of opera star.

Pavarotti and his manager opened the door to large-venue, stadiumlike events. During his American tours, Bocelli performed programs of opera music to crowds of fifteen thousand to twenty thousand per night. The Metropolitan Opera House, the biggest opera theater in the world, seats four thousand. The venues are not comparable, because stadium concerts are miked and the opera house delivers an entirely different experience.

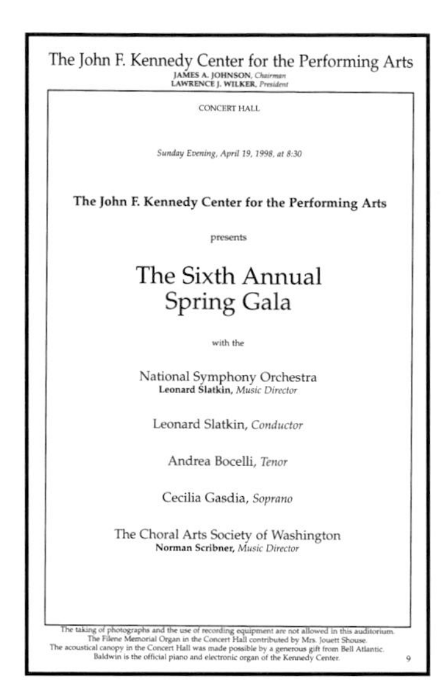

The John F. Kennedy Center for the Performing Arts
JAMES A. JOHNSON, *Chairman*
LAWRENCE J. WILKER, *President*

CONCERT HALL

Sunday Evening, April 19, 1998, at 8:30

The John F. Kennedy Center for the Performing Arts

presents

The Sixth Annual
Spring Gala

with the

National Symphony Orchestra
Leonard Slatkin, *Music Director*

Leonard Slatkin, *Conductor*

Andrea Bocelli, *Tenor*

Cecilia Gasdia, *Soprano*

The Choral Arts Society of Washington
Norman Scribner, *Music Director*

The taking of photographs and the use of recording equipment are not allowed in this auditorium.
The Filene Memorial Organ in the Concert Hall contributed by Mrs. Jouett Shouse.
The acoustical canopy in the Concert Hall was made possible by a generous gift from Bell Atlantic.
Baldwin is the official piano and electronic organ of the Kennedy Center.

9

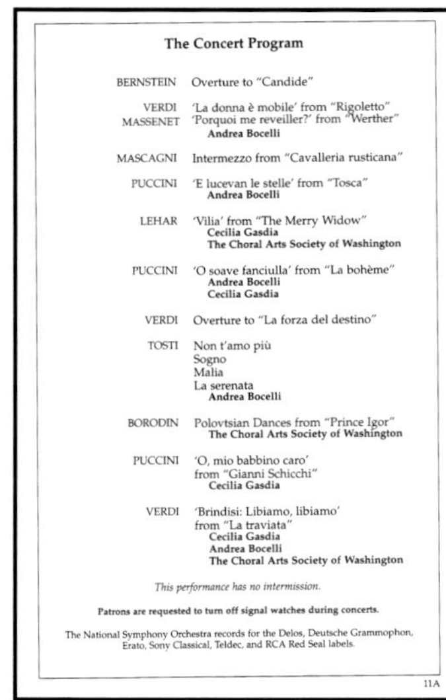

The Concert Program

BERNSTEIN Overture to "Candide"

VERDI 'La donna è mobile' from "Rigoletto"
MASSENET 'Porquoi me reveiller?' from "Werther"
Andrea Bocelli

MASCAGNI Intermezzo from "Cavalleria rusticana"

PUCCINI 'E lucevan le stelle' from "Tosca"
Andrea Bocelli

LEHAR 'Vilia' from "The Merry Widow"
Cecilia Gasdia
The Choral Arts Society of Washington

PUCCINI 'O soave fanciulla' from "La bohème"
Andrea Bocelli
Cecilia Gasdia

VERDI Overture to "La forza del destino"

TOSTI Non t'amo più
Sogno
Malia
La serenata
Andrea Bocelli

BORODIN Polovtsian Dances from "Prince Igor"
The Choral Arts Society of Washington

PUCCINI 'O, mio babbino caro'
from "Gianni Schicchi"
Cecilia Gasdia

VERDI 'Brindisi: Libiamo, libiamo'
from "La traviata"
Cecilia Gasdia
Andrea Bocelli
The Choral Arts Society of Washington

This performance has no intermission.

Patrons are requested to turn off signal watches during concerts.

The National Symphony Orchestra records for the Delos, Deutsche Grammophon, Erato, Sony Classical, Teldec, and RCA Red Seal labels.

11A

The program for Andrea Bocelli's American concert debut at the Kennedy Center for the Performing Arts in April 1998. One of America's most prestigious concert houses, this venue in Washington, D.C., is home to the National Symphony Orchestra conducted by Leonard Slatkin.

However, the repertoire of Bocelli's concerts is strictly opera except for a few popular encores. Bocelli's hope is that some of the people who have never heard opera before will go out and buy a copy of a full-length opera or go to the opera house.

Andrea Bocelli's concert debut in America took place a few months prior to his first big tour. On April 19, 1998, he shared the stage with Metropolitan Opera soprano Hei-Kyung Hong (who stepped in for the scheduled Cecilia Gasdia) in the Sixth Annual Spring Gala at the Kennedy Center for the Performing Arts in Washington, D.C. The two singers shared a program of arias and duets by Puccini, Verdi, Massenet, and Lehár, and Andrea also performed a set of Neapolitan songs by Tosti. Presenting himself to America in one of the country's most prestigious concert houses, Bocelli sang with the National Symphony Orchestra under the direction of Leonard Slatkin. The mixed reviews included one particularly nasty essay by David Patrick Stearns in *USA Today* that defines Bocelli's appeal as a result of the "David Helfgott effect," alluding to another musician with a disability. In spite of having observed the crowd's "rapturous" reaction, the critic describes Bocelli as "an amateur tenor with high notes" who was "uninspired" in his performance. Ken Ringle, however, writing for the *Washington Post*, was more impressed: "He was obviously nervous and vocally tight, and loosened up only moderately as the evening progressed, despite some radiant high notes. . . . But Bocelli's is an amazing voice nonetheless. It is a far younger, smaller, and even more boyish voice than Pavarotti's at the same age, but it carries a soulful purity that is absolutely mesmerizing in its upper registers."

The day after the concert, Andrea and Enrica were guests of President Bill Clinton at the White House. Bocelli described Clinton as "a very kind, very simple man," and commented on the Monica Lewinsky scandal that was front-page news at the time. "If it would have occurred to talk about it, I confess that I would have expressed, on my part, a certain sense of solidarity [with the President]," said Bocelli. "Not so much because I thought, 'Who is the saint among you who should throw the first stone?' but because it seemed to me—I'm not a politician, I don't understand politics—but it seemed to me a fact that was fabricated for political reasons. It was very sad."

Bocelli met the President again in May, 1999, when he sang at a Democratic Party fund-raiser in Hollywood. The event was sponsored by longtime Clinton supporter Steven Spielberg and attended by stars such as Meg Ryan and her husband Dennis Quaid, Rob Reiner, Whoopi Goldberg, Kirk Douglas, Goldie Hawn and Kurt Russell. Accompanied by Carlo Bernini, Andrea sang five arias out on the open-air terrace. Later in the evening, to everyone's surprise, he returned to the piano and accompanied himself to "My Way," to which the President and the rest of the crowd listened in rapt silence.

Andrea meets President Bill Clinton at the White House on April 19, 1998. The president invited both Andrea and Enrica to the White House the day following Andrea's debut concert at the Kennedy Center in Washington, D.C. "I've met persons like President Clinton and the Pope and many others," said Andrea, "persons with a kind of a charisma, who give me feelings which remain in me; I cannot explain it. Maybe I can say that the success has expanded my horizons."

Bocelli explained that he didn't participate in the fund-raiser for political reasons, but to repay the kindness of a man he admires. "I came here this evening for the man Clinton," Bocelli told the press, "not for the Democratic Party or their causes. I am here . . . because when I arrived in America the first time . . . I was received by Clinton at the White House, an honor that I believe is everyone's dream and that, as an Italian, filled me with great satisfaction." The photograph taken of the Bocellis with the President at the White House, blown up to nearly poster size, is prominently displayed in the living room of their home in Forte dei Marmi.

Three months after Bocelli's debut in Washington, D.C., he launched his first American tour at the Pittsburgh Civic Center with the Pittsburgh Symphony conducted by Steven Mercurio. The eleven-city tour played at Madison Square Garden in New York City, the Quebec Colisée Arena and Montreal Molsen Center in Canada, Chicago's United Center, Boston's Civic Arena, and other huge stadiums. "It was phenomenal," said Ed Kasses, president of Princeton Entertainment, which produced the tour. "We were hopelessly sold out for several shows including Madison Square Garden. The tour's success was way beyond our expectations."

Soprano Ana Maria Martinez shared the stage with Andrea Bocelli on each of his tours, singing solo arias and joining the tenor in opera duets and "Time to Say Goodbye." The young Puerto Rican soprano, a graduate of Juilliard, began her professional career in a series of concerts with Plácido Domingo after winning the famous Spanish tenor's international voice competition. She has since gone on to an international opera career, with performances at the Vienna State Opera, Deutsche Opera Berlin, Opera Stuttgart, Los Angeles Opera, New York City Opera, Michigan Opera Theater, and other companies. Of her New Jersey concert with Bocelli the *Star-Ledger* wrote: "Martinez sang Mimì with great grace and charm, her voice's smooth surface revealing surprising depths. Few headline tenors would allow themselves to be so overmatched."

Martinez was already a fan of Andrea Bocelli when her agent arranged the tour appearances. She and her entire extended family of aunts, uncles, and cousins listened to his CDs and loved his voice. "We all felt that Andrea had this very special way of reaching people," she said, "this incredible beauty and open heart that you hear through his music. His voice just melts you. When I found out I was going to be singing with him, I was just looking forward to meeting him. 'Wow,' I thought, 'and I get to sing with him too!' " The two singers met in Pittsburgh for just two days of rehearsal with the Pittsburgh Symphony before the tour.

"I was very under the weather," recalled Ana Maria. "I got sick, and some wonderful doctors in Pittsburgh were able to help me beat the cold so I could actually go on. But before opening night I didn't sing the final rehearsal at all. But Andrea, without warning Steven [the conductor], sang all of my arias! It was so great! After singing 'O mio babbino caro' he turned to Steven and said, 'You know, I always wanted to do that.' He's got such a great sense of humor. He said, 'Well, here's my chance to sing all these soprano arias.' And of course everyone had a great time with that. He sang 'Mi chiamano Mimì,' from *La Bohème*, 'Un bel di' from *Madama Butterfly*, and both parts of the *Bohème* duet 'O soave fanciulla.'

Photo: J. F. Mastroianni Associates, Inc.

Soprano Ana Maria Martinez, who joined Andrea Bocelli in his tours of North and South America in 1998 and 1999. A native of San Juan, Puerto Rico, the internationally acclaimed young singer is a great admirer of her colleague, Bocelli. "He's always looking to grow," she said. "When you think he's got it all, what else could he possibly want? Well, he wants to be the best that he can be, and every day is a challenge for him to reach another level. Which is yet another example that we can all learn from him."

For 'Con te partirò,' which was his big number, he did both parts as well."

The orchestra got to rehearse the soprano's numbers in a rehearsal they would not soon forget, and everyone got a great first impression of Bocelli. He created a jolly, upbeat atmosphere and also made Ana Maria feel much better about bowing out of the rehearsal. "Bocelli made the rehearsal feel like we were all family," she said. In addition to his spontaneity and sense of humor, Andrea revealed to everyone that worked with him on the tour that he is a very genuine person and extremely easy to work with. "Andrea is a very gentle man," said Martinez, "very soft spoken and sensitive, and extraordinarily intelligent. He doesn't take any of his success for granted, and he's absolutely one of the most genuine people I've ever met. It's a joy to speak with him and sing with him."

Martinez described the wild reactions from the crowds at every packed stadium. "I've done outdoor venues with Domingo, but I'd never done a venue for say fifteen or twenty thousand people like we did with Andrea. You feel the audience's love and adoration for him coming in waves toward the stage. It was so unlike anything else I've ever seen. People can admire a star and so forth, but this just goes beyond that. They go crazy. The only thing I think of is a Beatles concert. They're yelling their heads off and yelling his name: 'Andrea we love you! . . . Andrea come home with me!' Grown women just screeching, often with their husbands sitting next to them! It's a sight to behold.

"The feeling on these tours is always a very good one," she continued, "and I think it's because Andrea is so warm and easy to get along with. He communicates that warmth with his art. You hear it in his voice, you feel it from him, and you have no choice . . . it's like he's got this key to unlock your heart and it's beautiful to see everyone's heart, one by one, opening up. You feel that on the stage."

In a touring production that involved a ninety-piece orchestra, 130 other personnel, four trailers, four buses, and chartered jets, the American tour was a huge enterprise. Andrea spent most of his offstage time with his wife and two sons. Backstage and during some of the traveling, Martinez, who speaks Italian, chatted with Enrica and played with the boys. "Enrica definitely had her hands full with both children," she said. "She's very lovely, she always has a beautiful smile, no matter what's happening, which is very comforting. She takes everything with a grain of salt. She's a real natural beauty; I don't think I've ever seen her wear makeup, she doesn't need it. She's just one of those Mediterranean beauties who's very captivating. Amos, their older son, is such a character—very intelli-

"ANDREA IS SO WARM AND EASY TO GET ALONG WITH. HE COMMUNICATES THAT WARMTH WITH HIS ART. YOU HEAR IT IN HIS VOICE, YOU FEEL IT FROM HIM, AND YOU HAVE NO CHOICE . . . IT'S LIKE HE'S GOT THIS KEY TO UNLOCK YOUR HEART AND IT'S BEAUTIFUL TO SEE EVERYONE'S HEART, ONE BY ONE, OPENING UP. YOU FEEL THAT ON THE STAGE."
—*Ana Maria Martinez*

gent, very talkative, and with a great imagination." She recalled that Andrea did everything he could to give his sons a memorable experience of America. "He loves America," said Martinez. "He often said that he had never imagined how warm the American audiences would be. He was very moved by that."

The spring 1999 tour was completely sold out before it began in every location, including the Hollywood Bowl. During this concert Bocelli received a special visit from Elizabeth Taylor, a huge fan who had also attended his New Year's Eve concert in Las Vegas.

Bocelli's popularity in South America and other Spanish-speaking countries has grown with his tour appearances and with recordings such as *Sueño,* the Spanish version of *Sogno.* He introduced Portuguese pop singer Dulce Pontes to a huge new audience with their duet "O mare e tu" on *Sogno,* and has expressed a desire to record more Spanish-language music in the future. Bocelli is particularly fond of the songs of Brazilian composers Antonio Carlos Jobim and Toquinho. "I've always been a lover of Brazilian music and its

Andrea Bocelli onstage at Madison Square Garden in New York City during his summer 1998 American tour. Steven Mercurio is on the podium conducting the Pittsburgh Symphony Orchestra.

famous classics like 'The Girl from Ipanema,' he said. During a concert tour in Argentina, Bocelli described his attraction to and affection for that country: "Argentina and Italy are very much alike: the people are warm, very passionate. I am not saying this because of the people who attended my concerts, but because of what I received from the people in the streets, in the bars, in the embraces. The three things that touch me [here] are altruism, the ability to take care of people, and suffering."

In November 1998, Bocelli's United States exposure reached a new peak when he appeared in Celine Dion's holiday special, "These Are Special Times," on CBS. Andrea and Celine had met in Bologna a few months earlier, and hit it off immediately. "We met in a beautiful restaurant," said Andrea. "The feeling was immediate, one of those emotions that starts with a bang and you don't know why. . . . After five minutes we were almost friends and at the end of the lunch I was sure to sing with her because she was so nice—a beautiful woman—inside and outside, I think," said Andrea. The two singers then recorded the duet "The Prayer" by David Foster and Carol Bayer-Sager for the sound track to the animated film *Quest for Camelot*, and performed the song on Celine's television special. The TV show, aired on Thanksgiving, had the highest rating of any show on television that night and prompted huge sales of Bocelli's albums in the following days. *Romanza* had a fifty-eight-percent gain in sales and Aria sales shot up sixty-eight percent. Hitching his star to Celine Dion brought Andrea Bocelli legions of new fans plus a special new friendship based on "a sacred spark." He identifies with her hardworking attitude and desire to constantly improve. "Celine Dion for me is a very interesting singer because she thinks of her voice always," Bocelli said. "Every day she studies, she wants to improve. She thinks of her voice like an instrument." The admiration is mutual. "I fell in love with Andrea the first moment I saw him," said Celine Dion. "I wanted to meet him in person when I knew that I would share with him what I love most in the world—my music—and I remain touched by our first meeting. . . . Andrea is unbelievable. Perhaps he doesn't see with his eyes, but he feels and sees with his hands, his breath, his body. He holds it all under perfect control. He is sure of himself and he's happy."

With a vibe that seemed to permeate the airwaves, "The Prayer" carried Andrea Bocelli and Celine Dion to three more televised events within the next few months. First to the 1999 Golden Globes, in which Andrea participated via satellite from Tel Aviv, where he was recording *La Bohème* with Zubin Mehta. "The Prayer" won the Golden Globe for the best original song. Then on to the Grammy Awards in February 1999 in Los Angeles where Andrea Bocelli had been nominated for "Best New Artist." In this category he competed with Lauryn Hill, the Backstreet Boys, the Dixie Chicks, and Natalie Imbruglia. The Grammy went to Lauryn Hill, who swept the show with four additional Grammies that night. The night was not a failure for Bocelli, however. His passionate solo performance of "Amor ti vieta" from Umberto Giordano's opera *Fedora* and his duet with Celine Dion in "The Prayer" were met with standing ovations, and the television audience included a large percentage of MTV fans who had not heard him before. It was a big night for Celine Dion, who won the top award, Record of the Year, for "My Heart Will Go On" from the *Titanic* sound track. This song also gave her two more wins, for Song of the Year

Dulce Pontes, the Portuguese singer who performs the duet "O mare e tu" with Andrea on the albums Sogno *and its Spanish-language version,* Sueño. *They are pictured here in May 1999 during the ceremony commemorating* Sueño *going gold (selling over 50,000 copies).*

and Best Female Pop Vocal Performance.

Dion and Bocelli performed "The Prayer" for their biggest television audience yet at the Academy Awards in March 1999. That night Bocelli was truly a global star, performing with Dion before a television audience of more than two billion people. The winning Oscar went to another animated film song, "When You Believe," from *The Prince of Egypt*, recorded by Whitney Houston and Mariah Carey, who also performed it on the program.

Andrea Bocelli didn't have to go home to an empty awards shelf. In the spring of 1998 he won two trophies at the World Music Awards in Monte Carlo: Best-selling Italian Artist for *Romanza*, and Best-selling Classical Artist for *Viaggio Italiano*. His friend, Zucchero, had won for Best-selling Italian Artist

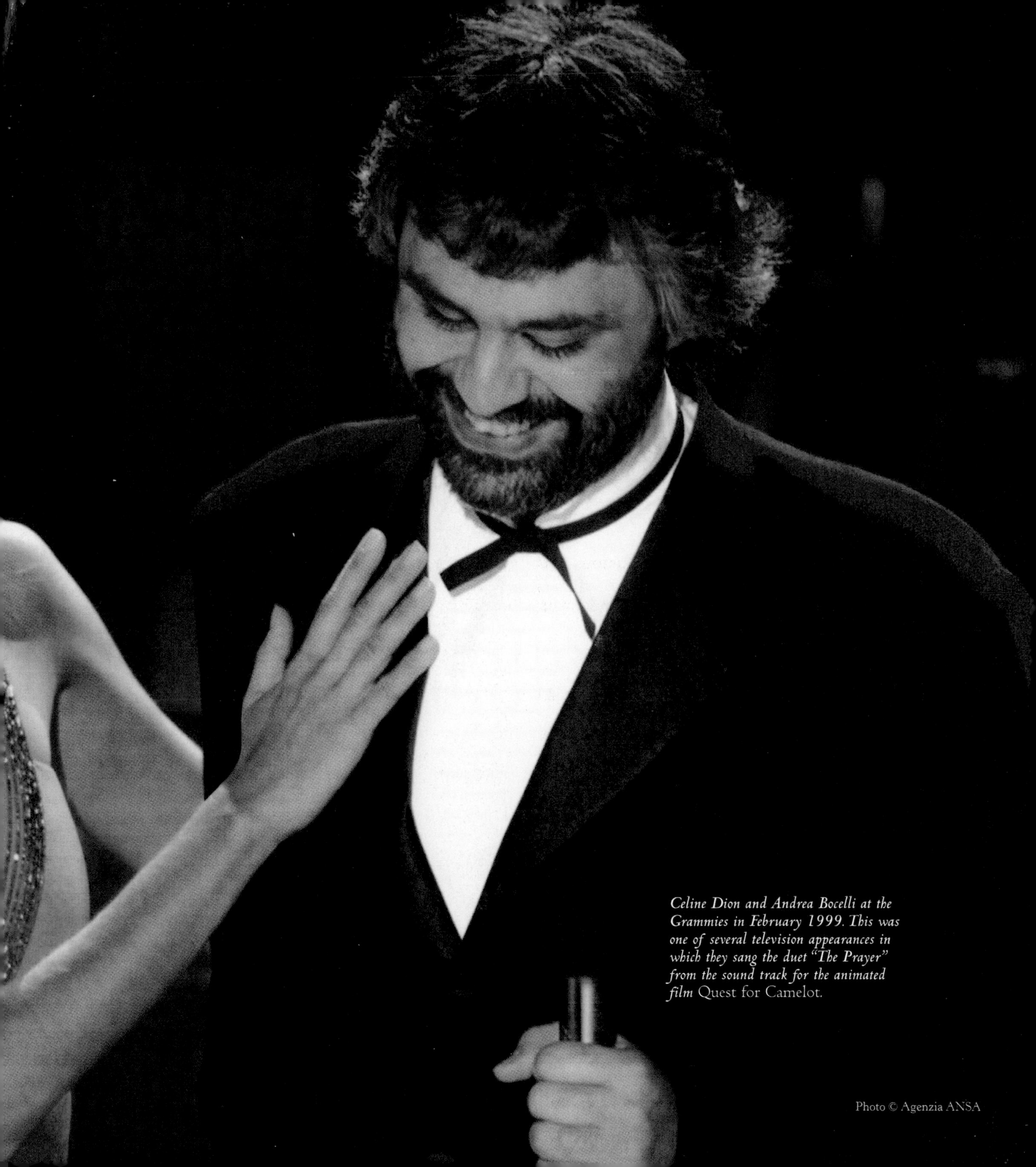

Celine Dion and Andrea Bocelli at the Grammies in February 1999. This was one of several television appearances in which they sang the duet "The Prayer" from the sound track for the animated film Quest for Camelot.

Photo © Agenzia ANSA

back in 1993. The World Music Awards are based on sales, and winners from other categories at the French Riviera event were the Spice Girls, Mariah Carey, Puff Daddy, and LeAnn Rimes. This glittering music award show is seen by five hundred million viewers worldwide in 130 countries. In 1997, Andrea Bocelli and Sarah Brightman received the U.K.'s Golden Disc Award for their single, "Time to Say Goodbye," and in Germany this duet won them the Echo Award for best-selling single. In the autumn of 1997, *Viaggio Italiano* received two awards in Germany, the Bambi Award for Best Classic CD and the Klassic Echo award.

Following up on the skyrocketing success of *Romanza* in the United States, PolyGram released Bocelli's fifth album, *Aria,* in 1998 and *Sogno* in 1999. Bocelli's string of national and international television appearances in early 1999—including talk shows such as *The Tonight Show with Jay Leno*—helped make *Sogno* an instant best-seller at the top of the charts in several countries, including the United States.

In *Opera News, Opera Now,* and other glossy magazines, famous sopranos, mezzos, and tenors have traditionally graced sumptuously photographed advertisements for Rolex watches. As a promoter of various products, Andrea Bocelli skipped over magazine ads and went straight to the airwaves. Bocelli's trademark song, "Con te partirò," has brought him remarkable glory and riches. In Italy, a cell-phone-toting Bocelli sings it in a television commercial for the phone company TIMM; and in Las Vegas, Nevada, it was used for a highly popular Bellagio hotel radio advertisement. Bellagio received so many calls about the song that PolyGram put stickers on the *Romanza* CDs and cassettes to signify that the song was included on the playlist. The hotel eventually hired Bocelli for a two-night, sold-out concert series on New Year's Eve and New Year's Day, 1999.

Andrea Bocelli's success, whether measured by wealth, celebrity, commercial output, or personal victory, has drastically altered his life. A hectic schedule of concerts, recordings, and benefit appearances has stripped him of his dearly held principle of never planning beyond twenty-four hours. "I've lost my privacy, my liberty," he said in March 1999. "Before, I planned my day each morning. Now I cannot live in such a way any longer; my days are planned for months and months." He is quick to add, however, that the sacrifices are worth it. He has even begun to embrace a few of the possibilities that dangle in the future, such as a blockbuster concert of "Three Divas and a Tenor" with Barbra Streisand, Whitney Houston, and Celine Dion. Or a movie with Franco Zeffirelli. Or, maybe best of all, singing "The Hymn of the 2000 Holy Year" at the ceremonious opening of the Basilica doors in Vatican City to usher in the holy year 2000, a Jubilee of the Catholic Church.

For Andrea Bocelli, anything is possible, and each day is a new opportunity to put something good into the world. "Classical music helps the spirit," he said. "It helps your soul to expand. As we get closer to the year 2000, life becomes more frenetic. Emotion gets lost. Music helps us recapture that emotion.

"Everyone has a voice," he added. "And I want to be a voice in the world."

Bocelli picked up two trophies at the 1998 World Music Awards in Monte Carlo. Romanza *won in the category of Best-selling Italian Artist and* Viaggio Italiano *for Best-selling Classical Artist.*

Photo © AP/Wide World Photos/Lionel Cironneau

DISCOGRAPHY

CDs

SOGNO (March 1999; Philips)

1. Canto della Terra
2. The Prayer (with Celine Dion)
3. Sogno
4. O Mare e Tu (with Dulce Pontes)
5. A Volte iI Cuore
6. Cantico
7. Mai Più Così Lontano
8. Immenso
9. Nel Cuore Lei (with Eros Ramazzotti)
10. Tremo e T'Amo
11. I Love Rossini
12. Un Canto
13. Come un Fiume Tu
14. A Mio Padre

SUEÑO (April 1999; PolyGram Latino)
The Spanish version of SOGNO containing three songs in Spanish

1. Canto de la Tierra
2. The Prayer (with Celine Dion)
3. Sueño
4. El Mar y Tu (with Dulce Pontes)
5. A Volte il Cuore
6. Cantico
7. Mai Più Così Lontano
8. Immenso
9. Nel Cuore Lei
10. Tremo e T'Amo
11. I Love Rossini
12. Un Canto
13. Come un Fiume Tu
14. A Mio Padre

ARIA: THE OPERA ALBUM
(April 1998; Philips)

1. *Rigoletto*: Questa o quella
2. *La Bohème* (Puccini): Che gelida manina
3. *Tosca*: Recondita armonia
4. *Tosca*: E lucevan le stelle
5. *Madama Butterfly*: Addio, fiorito asil
6. *Andrea Chenier*: Come un bel dì di maggio
7. *I Puritani*: A te, o cara
8. *Der Rosenkavalier*: Di rigori armato il seno
9. *Fedora*: Amor ti vieta
10. *La fanciulla del West*: Ch'ella mi creda
11. *La Gioconda*: Cielo e mar!
12. *Adriana Lecouvreur*: La dolcissima effigie
13. *La Bohème* (Leoncavallo): Musetta!—Testa adorata
14. *Lucia di Lammermoor*: Tombe degli avi miei—Fra poco a me ricoverò
15. *Werther*: Pourquoi me réveiller
16. *Carmen*: La fleur que tu m'avais jetée
17. *La Fille du Régiment*: Pour mon âme

ROMANZA (September 1997; Philips)
(version with 5 Spanish songs also released by Philips)

1. Con Te Partirò
2. Vivere
3. Per Amore
4. Il Mare Calmo della Sera
5. Caruso
6. Macchine da Guerra
7. Le Tue Parole
8. Vivo per Lei
9. Romanza
10. La Luna Che Non C'è
11. Rapsodia
12. Voglio Restare Così
13. E Chiove
14. Miserere/Live
15. Time to Say Good-bye (Con Te Partirò)

VIAGGIO ITALIANO
(October 1997; Philips)

1. *Turandot*: Nessun dorma
2. *L'Arlesiana*: Lamento di Federico
3. *Macbeth*: Ah, la paterna mano
4. *Rigoletto*: Le donna è mobile
5. *L'Elisir d'Amore*: Una furtiva lagrima
6. Panis Angelicus
7. Ave Maria
8. O Sole Mio
9. Core n'grato
10. Santa Lucia Luntana
11. I' Te Vurria Vasa
12. Tu, 'ca Nun Chiagne!
13. Marinarello
14. Piscatore 'e Pusilleco
15. Messaggio Bocelli (Message Bocelli)
16. Adeste Fideles (bonus track)

(Continued)

BOCELLI (1995/reissued 1998; Musicrama)

1. Con Te Partirò
2. Per Amore
3. Macchine da Guerra
4. E Chiove
5. Romanza
6. The Power of Love
7. Vivo per Lei
8. Le Tue Parole
9. Sempre Sempre
10. Voglio Restare Così
11. Vivo per Lei/Ich Lebe für Sie

IL MARE CALMO DELLA SERA
(1994/reissued 1998; Musicrama)

1. Il Mare Calmo della Sera
2. Ave Maria, No Morrò
3. Vivere
4. Rapsodia
5. La Luna Che Non C'è
6. Caruso
7. Miserere
8. Panis Angelicus
9. Ah, la Paterna Mano
10. E Lucevan Le Stelle
11. La Fleur Que Tu M'Avais Jetée
12. L'Anima Ho Stanca
13. Sogno

APPEARANCES ON OTHER CDs

ROMANTIC NIGHTS
(April 1999; RCA Victor)
Bocelli: "La Luna"

GRAMMY NOMINEES 1999
(February 1999; Elektra)
Bocelli: "Amor Ti Vieta"

HYMN FOR THE WORLD 2
(November 1998; Deutsche Grammophon)
Bocelli: "I Believe"

UN COEUR DE VERRE (Hélène Segara)
(December 1997; Musicrama)
Bocelli: "Je Vis pour Elle" (duet)

HYMN FOR THE WORLD
(November 1997; Deutsche Grammophon)
Bocelli: "Agnus Dei"

***QUEST FOR CAMELOT*: Music from the Motion Picture** [SOUNDTRACK]
(May 1998; Wea/Atlantic/Curb)
Bocelli: "The Prayer" (duet)

THESE ARE SPECIAL TIMES: CELINE DION (November 1998; Sony)
Bocelli: "The Prayer" (duet)

THE GREATEST OPERA SHOW ON EARTH (September 1997; London Classics)
Bocelli: "Mattinata"

EROS (Eros Ramazzotti) (1997; BMG)
Bocelli: "Musica è" (duet)

PAVAROTTI AND FRIENDS 2
(June 1995; London Classics)
Bocelli: "Mattinata"

VIDEO

A NIGHT IN TUSCANY (1997)
PolyGram Video

SOURCES

INTERVIEWS

Edi Bocelli	Marcello Garofalo	Beatrice Meucci
Vania Cenzatti	Leslie Jones	Stefano Paperini
Claudio Desderi	Lorenzo Malfatti	William Riley
David DiChiera	Ana Maria Martinez	John Sanfilippo
Anthony Falaro	Steven Mercurio	

BOOKS

Blau, Edouard, Milliet, Paul, and Hartmann, Georges. *Werther* (libretto). New York: G. Schirmer, 1968.

Caruso, Dorothy. *Enrico Caruso*. Westport, Conn.: Greenwood Press, 1945.

Domingo, Plácido. *My First Forty Years*. New York: Viking Penguin, 1984.

Fucito, Salvatore, and Beyer, Barnet J. *Caruso and the Art of Singing*. New York: Dover Publications, 1995.

Hines, Jerome. *Great Singers on Great Singing*. New York: Proscenium Publishers, 1990.

Hoelterhoff, Manuela. *Cinderella & Company*. New York: Knopf, 1998.

Jung, Carl Gustaf. *The Spirit in Man, Art, and Literature*. Princeton: Princeton University Press, 1966.

Krolick, Bettye. *Dictionary of Braille Music Signs*. Washington, D.C.: National Library Service, 1979.

Léon, Citor M., and Stein, Leo. *The Merry Widow* (libretto). New York: Souvenir Book Publishers, 1977.

Lewis, Marcia. *The Private Lives of the Three Tenors*. Secaucus, N.J.: Carol Publishing Group, 1996.

Osborne, Charles. *Verdi: A Life in the Theatre*. New York: Knopf, 1987.

Pavarotti, Adua. *Life with Luciano*. New York: Rizzoli, 1992.

Pavarotti, Luciano, with Wright, William. *Pavarotti: My World*. New York: Crown Publishers, 1995.

Robinson, Francis. *Celebration: The Metropolitan Opera*. New York: Doubleday, 1979.

Rossi, Nick. *Opera in Italy Today*. Portland, Ore.: Amadeus Press, 1995.

Schoep, Arthur and Harris, Daniel. *Word-by-Word Translations of Songs and Arias, Part II—Italian*. Metuchen, N.J.: The Scarecrow Press, 1972.

Spanner, H. V. *Lessons in Braille Music*. Louisville: American Printing House for the Blind, 1961.

Supervielle, Jules. *Selected Poems and Reflections on the Art of Poetry*. New York: Sun, 1985.

Wilson, Conrad. *Giacomo Puccini*. London: Phaidon Press, 1997.

ARTICLES/TRANSCRIPTS

Amusement Business, August 17, 1998; April 12, 1999

ANSA Italian News Service, June 23, 1999

Australian Women's Weekly, June 1999*

Billboard, December 12, 1998

Boston Herald, July 31 1998

Bunte, May 6, 1999*

Christian Science Monitor, February 20, 1998

Clarin, April 6, 1999*

Construire, April 15, 1998*

Corriere della Sera, February 19, 1998; August 3, 1998*

CTV, April 22, 1999, transcript: Bocelli.net

Das Neue, November 15, 1997*

Exclusive Weekend, June 1997*

Famiglia Cristiana, March 28, 1999*

Figaro, Le, March 27, 1999*

Frau mit Herz, July 1997*

Gala, January 1998*

Gazzetta, La, October 17, 1994*

"Good Morning America," July 21, 1998, transcript: Bocelli.net

GRTV, April 15, 1998*

Hollywood Reporter, May 4, 1999

Independent, June 18, 1997*

Los Angeles Times, October 8, 1998; December 10, 1998

Lourdes Magazine, N. 67, 68, 1999

Lundi, Le, January 17, 1998*

Mail on Sunday, March 28, 1999*

Music & Media, January 24, 1998; February 21, 1998; April 24, 1999

Nacion, La, November 8, 1997; May 3, 1999*

New York Newsday, March, 1999

New York Times, October 4, 1997; June 23, 1998; August 8, 1998; May 2, 1999; August 4, 1999

Oggi, March 31, 1999; May 12, 1999

Opera News, June 1994

Ottawa Sun, July 23, 1998*

Panorama, May 27, 1999*

Paris Match, December 20, 1997*

People Weekly, May 11, 1998

Public Broadcasting Report/Warren Publishing, April 10, 1998

RAITRE, "Una Vita in Musica," November 9, 1998, transcript: Bocelli.net

Reforma, May 31, 1998*

Repubblica, La, August 16, 1998*; November 10, 1998*; May 17, 1999*

Revista, La, November 30, 1997*

Story, February 20, 1997*

Tirreno, Il, September 27, 1994; plus various from archives 1993–1999

Unione Sardo, February 7, 1998*; February 15, 1998*; February 20, 1998*

USA Today, April 21, 1998

Vanidades, May 4, 1999*

Vedere Oltre, June 1999

Video Business, January 19, 1998

Wall Street Journal, December 8, 1997

Washington Post, April 26, 1998

Weekend, November 15, 1996*

* These articles were found on the Bocelli.net Web site.